how to groom your cat

Distributed in the U.S.A. by T.F.H. Publications, Inc., 211 West Sylvania Avenue, P.O. Box 27, Neptune City, N.J. 07753; in England by T.F.H. (Gt. Britain) Ltd., 13 Nutley Lane, Reigate, Surrey; in Canada to the book store and library trade by Clarke, Irwin & Company, Clarwin House, 791 St. Clair Avenue West, Toronto 10, Ontario; in Canada to the pet trade by Rolf C. Hagen Ltd., 3225 Sartelon Street, Montreal 382, Quebec; in Southeast Asia by Y.W. Ong, 9 Lorong 36 Geylang, Singapore 14; in Australia and the south Pacific by Pet Imports Pty. Ltd., P.O. Box 149, Brookvale 2100, N.S.W., Australia. Published by T.F.H. Publications Inc. Ltd., The British Crown Colony of Hong Kong.

how to
groom your cat

for beauty, health and show

with special emphasis
on longhaired cats

by
betty meins &
wanita floyd

t.f.h.

ISBN 0-87666-174-6

Co-author Betty L. Meins with Quad. Ch. Zoda Candace of La Cresta.

Co-author Wanita Floyd with Africat's Jungle Genii and Gr. Ch. Windsong Mystique of Africat.

Tr. Gr. Ch. Dorker's Peach Blossom of Isle of View, a shaded Cameo female. Doris Harris, breeder. Donna Norris and Barbara Fletcher, owners.

Octuple Gr. Ch. Lowland's Zeus of Lin-Lea, "All-American Cat of the Year" in 1971. A. D. Bandy, breeder. Mrs. Ralph Beery, Duarte, Calif., owner. A cream Persian male.

Gr. and Quad. Ch. Arista Char-Ming of Sai Ban, a blue point Siamese female, sired by Arista's Ti-Ci-Tu. Dam is Arista's Blue Sprite. Genevieve Scudder, San Diego, breeder. George Silva, Lemon Grove, Calif., owner.

DEDICATION

DEDICATED to all the cats who have loved us, taught us and guided us with loving purrs and paws, but most especially to . . .

The La Cresta cats:

Tpl. Ch. Battis Misty April of La Cresta
Quad Ch. Zoda Juliana of La Cresta
Dbl. Gr. Ch. Zoda Rose Parade of La Cresta
Dbl. Gr. Ch. La Cresta's Edelweiss
Quad Ch. La Cresta's Mardigras
Gr. Ch. La Cresta's White Robin
Quad Ch. Zoda Candace of La Cresta
La Cresta's Fidelity

The Africat cats:

Gr. Ch. Windsong Mystique of La Marque (Africat)
Dbl. Gr. Ch. La Marque's Greek Smoke (Africat)
Gr. Ch. La Marque's Angel Puss (Africat)
Quad Ch. La Marque's Tiki Nui (Africat)
Ch. La Marque's Koko Po Iki (Africat)
Africat's Puddy Tat
Africat's Jungle Genii
Africat's Diablo

Instructional photo credits to JACK ARNESON

Contents

Love the cat . . . not the Win

INTRODUCTION

It has often been said that what the world needs today is a good $1.98 psychiatrist. We of the cat fancy think what the world of the cat show needs is a Poor Richard's Handbook for the Helpless . . . for who is more helpless than the novice with his first lovely pedigreed cat! We hope to lead the reader through the growing pains of good grooming. If in addition to helping beginners we also remind the veteran cat show exhibitor of a tip or two he has forgotten, we will be pleased. But most important . . . we shall endeavor to help you help the lovely cats in your care, without which the world would be less than the delightful place we enjoy.

BETTY MEINS
WANITA FLOYD

1

HEALTH AND THE SHOW COAT

Since this book is primarily concerned with the well-groomed show cat, we must emphasize at this point that you must have a healthy animal that is producing a healthy coat in order to have anything to groom and show!

The physical condition of your show cat is vital to its appearance. The cat that is nutritionally underfed or in need of exercise and muscle tone or continually fighting off minor ailments cannot be expected to grow or retain a luxurious show coat. We do not mean to imply that the exhibitor of such a cat neglects his cattery, but rather that the over-indulgent crazy-about-that-cat owner might handicap his animal by treating it *too* well. All too often the show cat is restricted to a hothouse environment, avoiding any contact with clean fresh air which the doting owner is convinced will induce galloping pneumonia at first whiff. Kitty is permitted neither the freedom of an enclosed exercise yard nor the exertion of climbing and clawing her way to the top of a tall carpeted cat tree. Accident potential, you know, mustn't take chances! And heaven forbid that the adoring owner should force his cat to accept prescribed medicines or daily vitamins if kitty doesn't want them. It might disturb the feline psyche or something equally vague. We do not mean that you should not love your cats and spoil them silly if you like. Love is psychologically essential to any pet. What we do suggest is that you love them *enough* to do what is *best for them.*

PROPER DIET

One of the most important things in a show cat's life is his diet. Without proper diet, no cat can possibly reach his full potential of beauty or personality. Since the feline is primarily a carnivorous animal, a natural meat eater, we should understand the importance of fresh meat in his diet. Some catteries feed canned cat foods, but most adhere to a basic raw meat and dry food combination with vitamin/mineral additives. Most veterinarians recommend fresh meat a minimum of four out of seven days. Raw chunk meat should be fed occasionally to keep teeth and gums in good condition.

The authors feel the finest daily diet possible consists of the following:
(measurements shown in one-pound portions)

$\frac{3}{4}$ lb horsemeat, raw
$\frac{1}{4}$ lb beef, raw
salted lightly (iodized)
2 T. dry meal or small kibble
1 t. powdered brewers yeast (or comparable tablet)
1 t. vitamin/mineral supplement (powder form)
$\frac{1}{2}$ t. calcium lactate (powdered or liquid)
$\frac{1}{4}$ t. cod liver oil
add enough water to mix easily yet firmly
If horsemeat is not used, 1 teaspoon of tomato juice per adult cat per day should be added to the diet.

Heart, liver, chicken or kidney may be offered now and then to vary the taste and pique the appetite, but these meats should not be used as a single diet staple. Small pieces of the family roast or barbecued steak can be fed to the cat as an occasional treat. Fish (except red tuna, which should *never* be offered) may be offered on rare occasions but *never* red tuna or raw pork. Avoid bones of any size!

FEEDING AMOUNTS AND FREQUENCY

The amount you feed your cat depends upon both the breed and the habits of the individual cat. A fat animal is no healthier than a fat person. Certain breeds tend to be lean and muscular; others, especially the longhairs, are heavy-bodied. Active bouncy cats will consume more food than the passive beauty who spends most of her day dozing on a pillow. Breeders usually allow their longhair show cats to weigh a bit more during show season than during breeding season, but it is well to remember that the seriously overweight animal may have trouble conceiving as well as delivering her litter.

The time you feed your cats is best determined by your own schedule, but it is wise and healthier to feed him at the same time each day. Cattery owners generally agree that it is better to feed two meals a day than to leave food for nibbling. This is especially true of the cat who is a fussy eater or who disdains the nutritional portion of his diet. Never allow your cat to determine his own diet by what he likes best. You wouldn't allow your children to eat just ice cream and candy, so do not allow your show cat to choose only the temptation foods. A healthy show coat requires a healthy diet.

LIQUIDS

Fresh water must be available to your cats at all times. Breeders and veterinarians agree that male cats—whether whole or neutered—are generally healthier if given distilled water only. Cat show exhibitors frequently carry bottled water from home to insure an uninterrupted source of pure drinking water. The taste of unfamiliar chlorine or mineral content in out-of-town water will sometimes cause the show cat to do without water for an entire show weekend which might, under extreme or repetitious circumstances, cause urinary problems. Also, water with high mineral content can cause diarrhea.

PROPER FEEDING BOWLS

The new Persian owner quickly learns to feed kitty from a flat plate or saucer. Cats object to pushing their broad, flat faces down into a bowl. The flat surface allows cats to approach the food from the side, thereby avoiding the discomfort of burying their short noses at each bite and possibly obstructing their breathing. Picture yourself attempting to drink soup from the lower inch of a deep bowl without a spoon and you'll soon sympathize with kitty's flat-faced dilemma.

VITAMIN/MINERAL SUPPLEMENTS

Vitamin/mineral supplements are available in many forms and under many brands. You may prefer the

Products such as these are found in the pet stores and aid in the health and care of your cat.

powdered form designed to be stirred into kitty's food. Kitty, however, may or may not adjust to your preferences. She may prefer the plain or flavored tablet, or the one faintly scented with catnip, or perhaps a "straight shot" of liquid concentrate. There is even a vitamin/mineral supplement in a malt-flavored paste which comes in a handy extruded form that kitty licks off your finger. It is not the form in which your vitamins and minerals come that is important, but rather that they are given *regularly* and in the proper amount; directions are quite explicit on the labels. Use a reputable brand—one recommended by a successful show cattery or by your favorite veterinarian—rather than the bargain priced article in the supermarket. Extra calcium and pre-natal supplements are recommended for expectant mothers and nursing queens. Many breeders believe Vitamin C, in veterinarian-prescribed quantities, is successful in warding off winter colds and respiratory infections while simultaneously working as an acidifier for your cat. Wheat germ oil or Vitamin E may be given during breeding season.

PROPER EXERCISE

Exercise is vital for good health in any animal. The show cat, because it must be in top condition to show well, must be given the opportunity to run, jump and climb. Proper exercise firms muscle tone, increases the blood circulation around the hair follicles and improves the appetite. Cats allowed the freedom of the house and a floor-to-ceiling cat tree will usually solve the exercise problem themselves. Many show catteries, however, are of such size that the cats must be denied house privileges. Caged cats *must* be provided with jumping shelves, climbing posts and, ideally, an enclosed exercise run. Scratching posts should be securely fastened and cattery play area floors cleaned but not waxed. Enthusiastic play on a highly polished floor could easily result in a tragic accident. An outdoor exercise

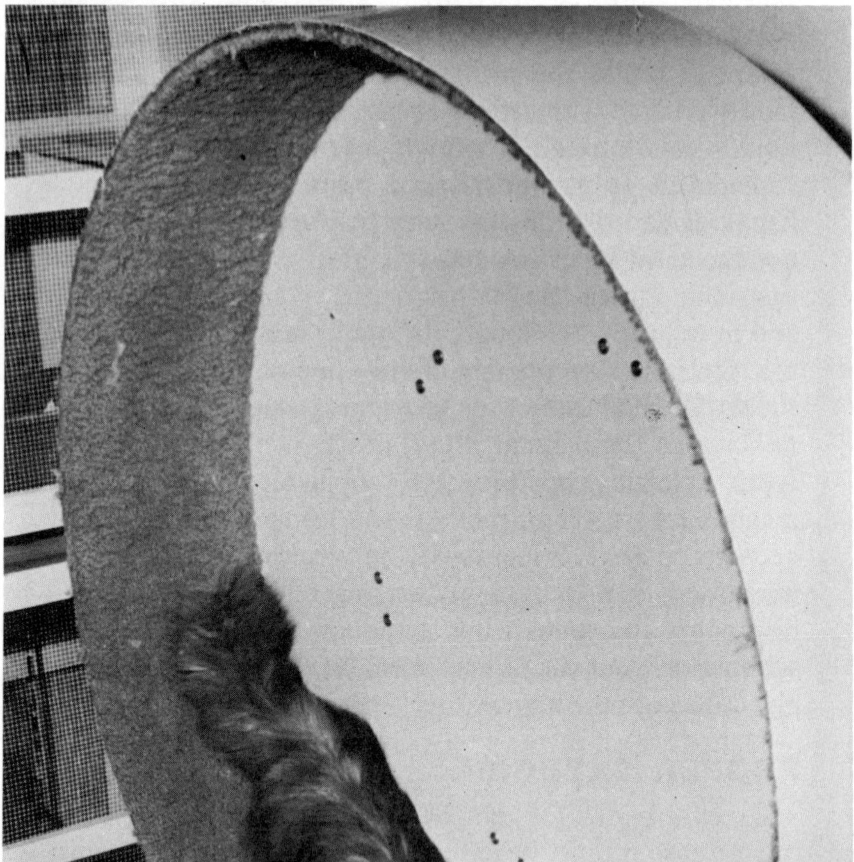

This indoor exercise wheel, custom built for La Cresta Cattery, is one-cat-powered and is a means for good daily exercise.

cage with both sun and shade areas provides a delightful interlude for the indoor cat. Take care, however, that the direct sunlight does not discolor the fragile show coat. With certain cats—blacks, smokes, creams and blues particularly—a shaded run should be provided.

The authors solved their indoor exercise problem with a unique cat wheel. The five-foot-high, free-standing wheel is one-cat powered and spins silently on ball bearings at the mere touch of a paw. The inner wheel surface is carpeted to provide secure footing for the galloping felines. Designed by Mrs. Meins and custom built for use in her cattery, the wheel has proved highly successful as an exercise medium.

Model outdoor cages containing jumping shelves and shady areas.

Cat toys are helpful incentives to exercise, especially for the pretty-on-a-pillow fat cat who disdains the ordeal of active exertion. Toys should be large enough not to be swallowed, yet small enough to be batted about in a game of chase-and-chomp. Avoid button eyes, edible-size bells and ribbons and decorations which might pull free during play. A ping-pong ball makes a particularly nice toy for the cat who needs muscle tone. One enthusiastic paw will send it bouncing harmlessly off the walls, with kitty in hot pursuit. Catnip-filled toys and mice are Number One in the Chase Parade, but did you know that some cats are

This indoor cage has tiled floor, scratching and climbing post, assortment of toys to keep kitty happy and healthy.

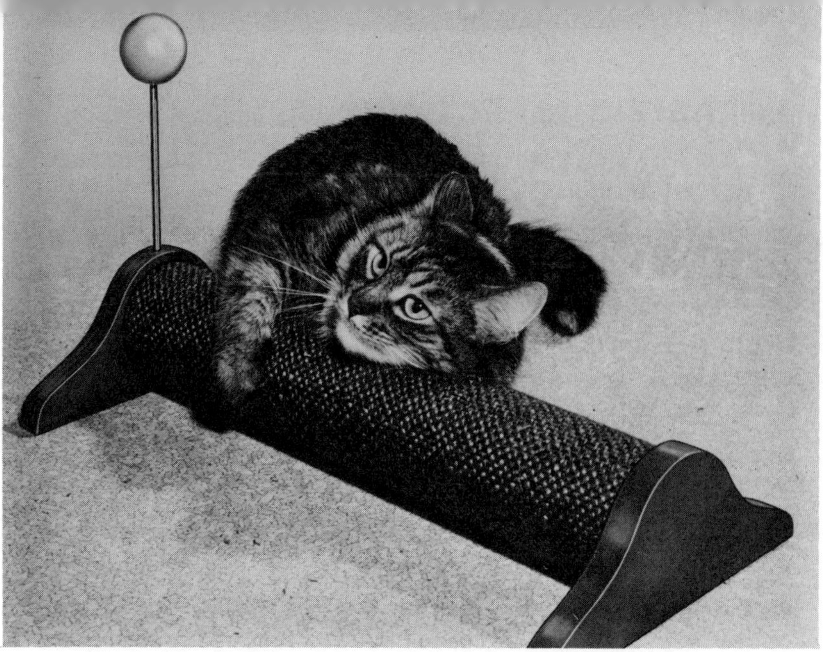

Love that cat bar!

allergic to catnip? Red or running eyes, sneezing when playing with catnip toys and similar catnip-timed symptoms should be carefully noted. If this occurs with one of your cats, take the toy away and wait until the problem clears up . . . then try again. If the symptom recurs, kitty has a problem and will just have to go on the catnip-wagon.

Never turn your cat loose outdoors! It is dangerous for any animal to run free in the city, but especially in the case of the show cat. A neighborly squabble with the tomcat next door could mean a torn ear and the unscheduled end of a successful show career. Also, indiscriminate mating might result in coat loss from the ruff, shoulders and sides as well as in unwanted litters. Oil on a driveway can stain a show coat for the entire season, not to mention the irreparable damage that can occur from spilled bleach in the laundry room. And worse, your lovely animal could be stolen or hit by a car. Show cats are not intended for freeways and friendly dog fights. Keep them restrained, safe and beautiful.

PARASITIC INFECTIONS

A healthy cat or kitten is one who is free of all parasites. Those which most frequently plague the show cat are worms, ear mites and fleas. Worms can sometimes be detected by feces examination in the litter pan, by vomiting or, most efficiently, by laboratory analysis of the fecal matter. If for any reason you suspect your cat of having worms, a *fresh* stool specimen should be taken immediately to your veterinarian, the type of worms determined and treatment effected. De-worming should always be done by a qualified veterinarian.

Ear mites are minute parasites that infest inside the ear. The mites themselves are so small as to be virtually invisible to the naked eye, but the irritation caused by their presence in the sensitive ear canal produces a dark crumb-

Nile's Menesa III, an Abyssinian female. Maureen Nottingham, owner-breeder.

Kitty should see her veterinarian once a year for a booster shot and check-up.

ling waxlike secretion which can be seen and is often mistaken for dirt. A microscopic examination by a vet will quickly verify the infestation. Since mites are readily passed from cat to cat, prompt treatment is suggested.

Despite best efforts, fleas "bug" every cat sooner or later. The cat with fleas will scratch . . . scratching causes loss of coat, matting and skin irritation . . . and there goes your show season snug as a bug in a Persian rug.

Dangerous diseases such as infectious anemia can be transmitted to your cat by fleas. They are hosts to tapeworm, and fleas can actually kill a very small kitten. Like taxes, they are hard to avoid . . . but not impossible. The most effective and safest products are available through your veterinarian, but there are many quality flea products in the pet stores as well. Know your brands and use only those products made *especially for cats.* Powders and sprays are made to use directly on the animal. The spray lasts longer, since it reaches deeper into the plush coat and has a residual action. Many cats are afraid of the hissing sound of the spray can and, therefore, powder products are more readily accepted. Since some sprays have an oil base which causes the hair to stick together and lay close to the body, de-flea your show cat well before show season. White flea powder should always be used on a white cat, because cream or off-white powder may discolor the stark white coat.

Flea collars are effective but very risky for show cats. They occasionally cause an allergenic skin eruption and most certainly will break off the ruff of the longhair cat. The thiamine B vitamin is believed to discourage fleas on cats, but there are also tablets to eat, liquids to spray in your yard and even flea-treated bedding materials. Pest strips have proved effective in many cases as a means of keeping fleas and bugs away from animal areas. They must be used exactly as directed and hung from the ceiling well out of the animal's reach. We suggest, however, that *all* such chemical products be approved by a veterinarian before its use in your area.

Any sign of parasites discovered in the vet line examination the day of the show may disqualify your cat from the show hall. Never permit the merest suspicion of parasites to go unchecked. A light infestation is quick and simple to treat, but when allowed to multiply, these parasites may require months or perhaps the entire show season to curb.

PREVENTIVE MEDICINE

The treatment of any illness, disease or parasitic infestation should be handled by a qualified veterinarian. Clip kitty's claws before each visit, record the date of each feline enteritis shot and take him in promptly for the annual booster. The cost of preventive medicine is nominal when compared to the cost of treating a long term illness. Ask your vet how to properly take kitty's temperature, and how to give pills and medications. He will appreciate your interest in the animal's continued good health. Furthermore, your vet will bargain with you—he won't show cats if you won't practice medicine.

Masampa-T. Francis, Brown Mackerel tabby longhair. An example of fine grooming of a household pet. Margaret Simmons, La Mesa, Calif., owner.

Dbl. Gr. and Tpl. Ch. La Cresta's Edelweiss, a copper-eyed white Persian female. Mrs. Betty L. Meins, breeder and owner.

2

GROOMING THE LONGHAIR CAT

Grooming the longhair cat as a pet is relatively simple, but grooming the longhair for a show is not an easy task, even for the experienced cat-lover. It requires a great deal of thought, year-round pre-planning, infinite patience, repetitious grooming, and much much time which your family may feel better spent elsewhere. It can also be a delightfully rewarding experience for the owner and cat, especially if the cat enjoys showing off.

The importance of year-round BASIC GROOMING should be impressed upon every cat owner. Keeping the longhair cat combed is important for three reasons: first, to keep him beautiful; second, to keep him mat-free and comfortable; and finally, to prevent the formation of hairballs in the stomach. While the longhair cat does not shed any more hair than the shorthair cat, the hair itself is much longer and, therefore, much more noticeable in your cat comb . . . and on the couch, and on the carpet, and on your best dark suit! Discounting the inconvenience of shedding hair, it can also be a detriment to your cat's health if consumed. In a natural effort to groom himself, the cat licks his coat, swallows the hair and becomes internally congested with hairballs. Again, prevention is the best medicine. Several suitable products—such as Petromalt, Femalt, etc.—aid in the elimination of hairballs and the coughing, vomiting and constipation they cause. Kit-Vite combines hairball prevention with a vitamin/

mineral concentrate, thereby solving two problems with one lick so to speak. The hairball problem is no less serious in shorthair cats, only less frequent, and preventive measures are recommended.

DAILY COMBING

Comb daily to prevent knotting of the long show coat. Never allow a knot to remain in the coat more than twenty-four hours if at all possible. The natural activity and movement of the cat will cause more and more hair to become tangled into the knot, and within a few days the snarl will have become a solid mat an inch or more in diameter and may require cutting out—*disaster* for the show cat and unattractive at best for the house pet!

The degree of knotting, or matting, as it is referred to by breeders, depends on the type, texture and length of the individual coat. Fine hair mats more quickly than coarse hair. It also varies with the season; the loss of dead hair in the spring causes greater mats at shorter intervals. Generally speaking, the coarse hair of the black, smoke Himalayan or the occasional white requires less combing than the unusually fine coat of the blue, cream and silver cat. There are exceptions, of course, for it is not the color but the texture that determines the severity of matting and the frequency of combing. Those fortunate cats who do not mat must, nevertheless, be combed regularly to remove dead hair and to preserve the "daily grooming ritual" to which he has grown passively accustomed.

MAT REMOVAL

The removal of mats is a relatively simple matter when carefully done with the proper tool. Dritz Seam Rippers, available at any sewing center, are lopsided "U"-shaped sewing tools with a protected but very sharp blade at the apex of the "U." They are invaluable to the longhair cat owner.

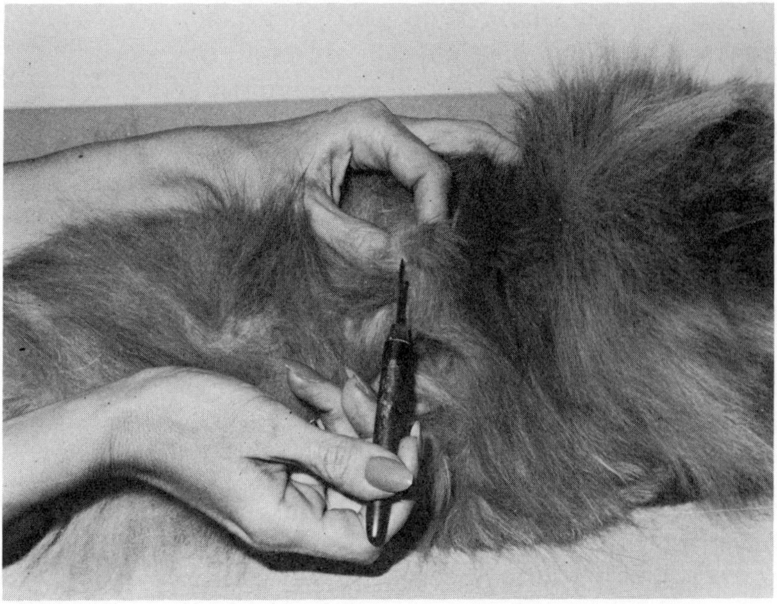

After having separated the mat into small sections, the Dritz Seam Ripper will then lift and free the hair without discomfort to the cat. Remember to guide the blade so as not to pierce the tender skin or rip the fragile hair.

Mats to be removed should first be separated into several small pieces by pulling them apart with the fingers. The Dritz Seam Ripper is then carefully inserted at the base of the knot, lifting the blade up and out. The blade frees the fragile hair without discomfort to the cat and without removing great chunks of the coat. Guard the point of the seam ripper with your finger as you insert the long end beneath the knot, taking great care not to scratch or pierce the skin. If you don't have a seam ripper, you may remove small mats by using the last one or two teeth of a grooming comb. *Never* put the whole comb into a matted area and just pull. It is too painful to the animal, it eliminates the cat's patience with future grooming attempts, and it ruins the show coat. "Pulling" out knots results in a cat who looks like the results of a five-year-old's debut at a barber college.

When all mats have been gently removed, comb once more . . . then offer kitty a special treat for being so patient. Daily combing takes only a few minutes and prevents unsightly mats and gaping holes in a once-lovely coat. Make grooming a pleasant interlude in your cat's day, but also impress upon him that grooming is *not* playtime. Never allow your show cat to play with the comb or implements. The time will surely come when such horse-play at a show will mean the difference between a win and a defeat. Be reassuring and gentle but be FIRM.

STUD TAIL GROOMING

Stud tail or grease tail is caused by overactive glands at the base of the tail and along the top side of the tail which secrete a heavy dark grease or waxlike substance.

Comb the stud tail area gently to avoid stimulation of the overactive tail glands.

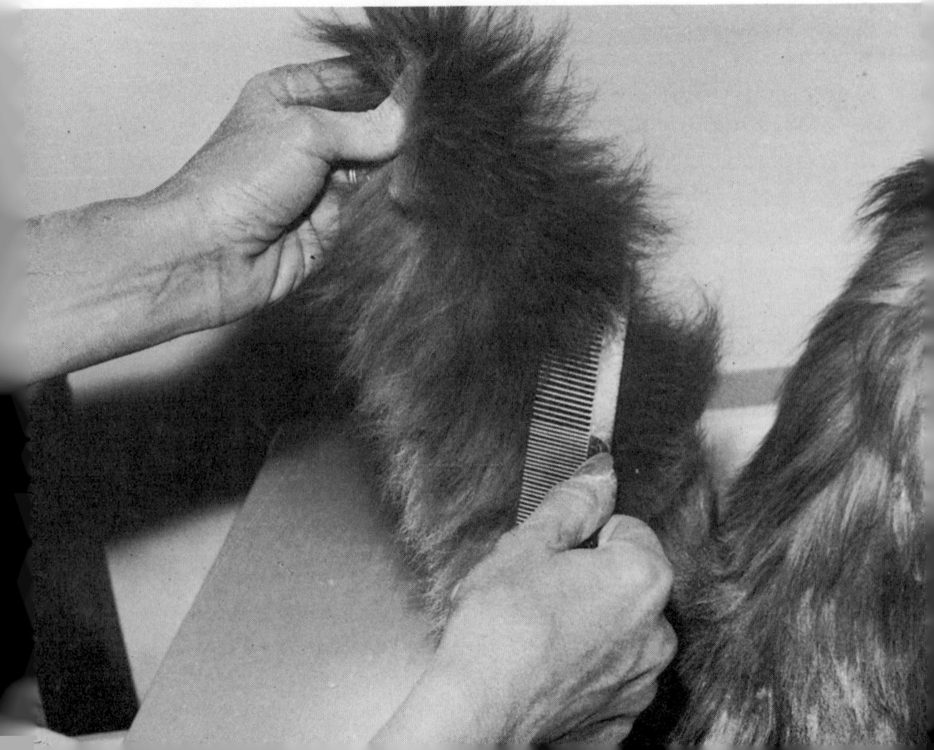

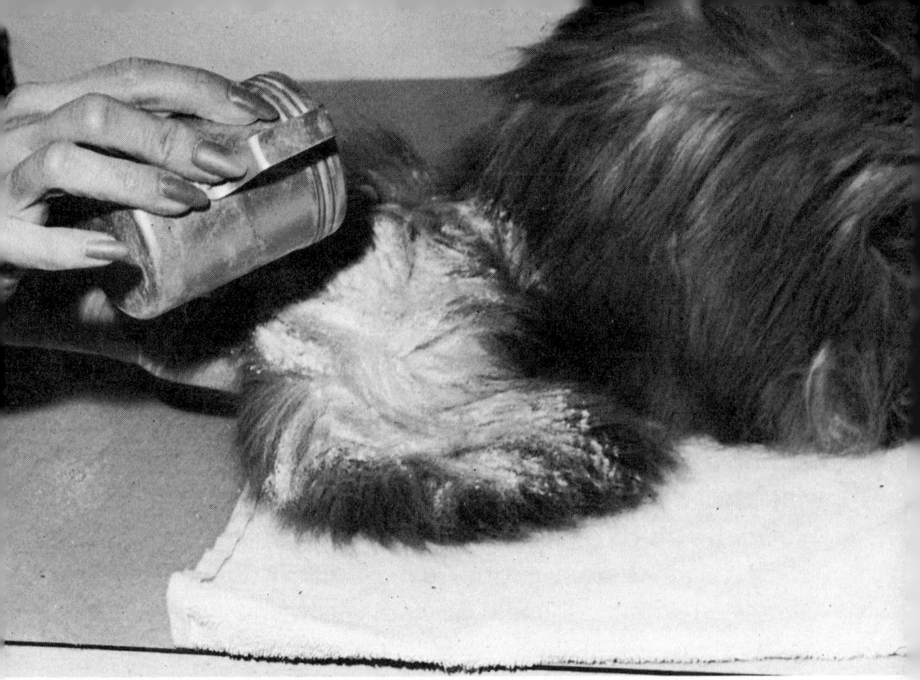

Powder the full length of the tail, giving special attention to the stud tail area by using a non-toxic germicidal powder at least once a week.

It occurs in cats of all breeds, ages, and both sexes, although whole breeding males seem to have more than their fair share of the unpleasant affliction. It is the curse of both cat and owner.

To cleanse wash the affected area with warm water and a *mild* detergent; the detergent cuts the grease from the tail in much the same manner as it removes the stubborn grease from a frying pan. Confine the use of detergent to the affected area to avoid unnecessary drying of the coat. Wash the area repeatedly with warm water, scrubbing the detergent right down to the skin with a round shoe brush or soft toothbrush. Allow the soap to remain on the skin for a moment or two—the cat's patience permitting—then rinse well. Repeat, if necessary, until the hair is squeaky clean. (In severe cases, where the skin is raw, Surgeon's Soap is recommended over detergent.) Towel dry and apply boric acid powder to the area while still damp. Work the powder well down into the hair and next to the skin. All powder must be blown out prior to show time if your are grooming your cat for the show.

Stud tail is not a problem to be dismissed lightly. Should the condition occur, the hair will become sticky and discolored. If the affected area is not properly cleansed and medicated, infection may set in, resulting in permanent damage to the hair follicles. Do not brush or massage the tail area; avoid undue stimulation. Comb only when required to groom or arrange the coat. Powder the stud tail area weekly with talcum, cornstarch or NP-27 Foot Powder, which combines the drying powder with an effective non-toxic germicide. If the problem is not alleviated with reasonable care, a visit to your veterinarian is in order.

When clipping kitty's nails, hold him steady so that a sudden squirm does not cause you to cut into the quick, the sensitive pink area at the base of the nail.

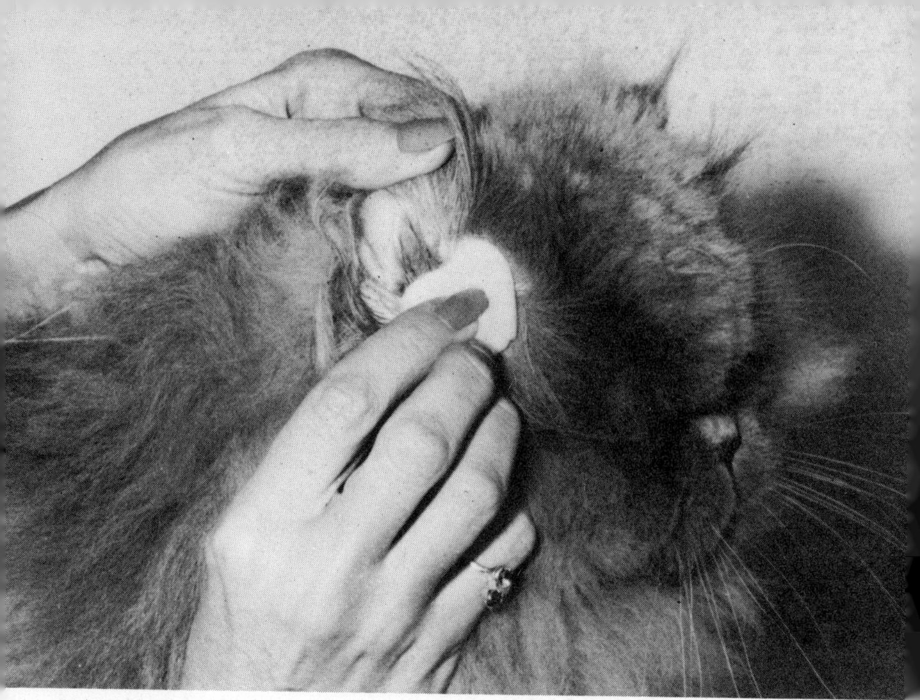

Should your cat's ear require cleaning, a Q-tip slightly moistened with mild soap can be rubbed gently over the dingy surfaces, but only as deep as the eye can see.

NAIL CLIPPING

Nail clipping is one of the *essential* steps in the grooming procedure. Special cat nail clippers may be purchased at any pet shop. Nail clipping should begin in kittenhood and be repeated at regular intervals throughout the year. If you prefer, clip front feet only for "at home" cats but clip all four feet for show cats. As a courtesy to the judges, *always* clip the show cat's claws the day before a show.

The foot is held in one hand, gently pressing on the middle of the foot with thumb and forefinger to extend the claws fully. Only the transparent tip or curl of the claw should be removed. To prevent splintering and splitting of the claw, clippers should be held sideways so that they cut from *both* sides of the nail, rather than from top to bottom. Never clip too deeply. "Quicking" of the nail can result in soreness and possible infection.

SPECIAL EAR CARE

Cleaning the ears of a healthy cat presents little problem as a rule. Most cats do a pretty good job all by themselves. Some cats, like some people, secrete more wax than others, and the excess wax picks up dirt and dust to give the inner ear a dingy, unkempt appearance.

Cleanse the ear with a bendable Q-tip or piece of cotton dipped in warm water and rubbed lightly with mild soap (such as Johnson's Baby Soap or Neutrogena). Rub the Q-tip gently over the visible surfaces of the inner ear, taking great care not to drip water into the ear and not to go any deeper than you can see. Especially stubborn ear wax stains may require a little Labco Dry Cleaner on the Q-tip. Be especially careful during show season, if you want to show your cat, not to dirty the long ear tufts with wax as it is removed. Should the tufts become soiled, wash immediately with warm water and mild soap or Labco to prevent permanent stain.

Digging or scratching at the ears indicates the possible presence of ear mites; an immediate visit to your veterinarian is recommended.

EYE STAIN REMOVAL

Eye stain is a common problem among longhair cats, particularly the snub-nosed Persian, even when perfectly healthy. The shorter the nose and the more pronounced the nose break, the more the eyes seem to tear. The tears collect on the face and darken into tear-lines on the cheeks. Tear stain should be removed daily with a bit of cotton to prevent build-up.

Cleanse the tear stain area gently with cotton dampened with warm water, then pat dry with fresh cotton. Stubborn stains may require the assistance of a commercial eye stain remover and/or the application of eye chalk stick. At the show hall, a piece of dry cotton should be used to brush away any sign of dampness as soon as it appears in

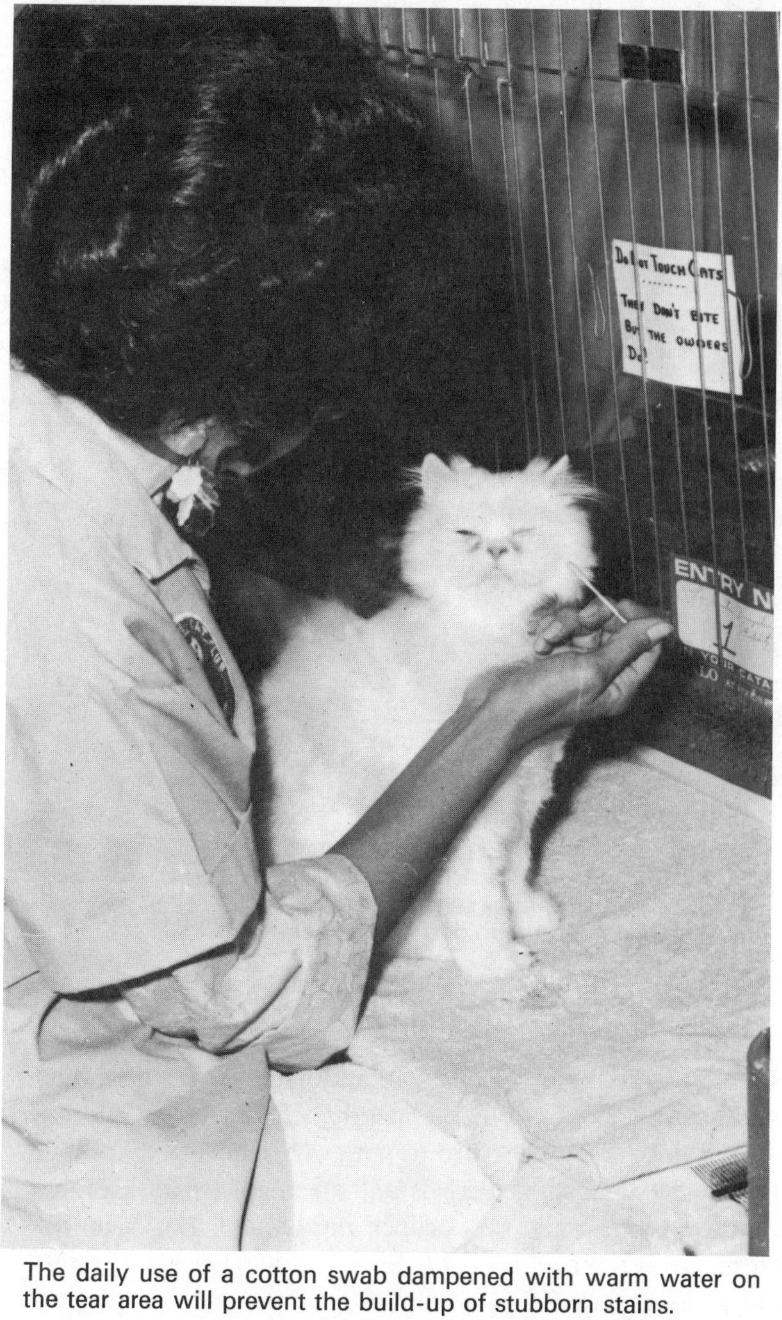

The daily use of a cotton swab dampened with warm water on the tear area will prevent the build-up of stubborn stains.

order to be immediately ready for the judge's call. If needed, cornstarch may be used to dry the area, but avoid the use of grooming powder too close to the eyes.

For dust-reddened or travel-tired eyes, a drop or two of Visine (or similar non-toxic preparation for cats) will put sparkle in the eyes for an on-the-spot miracle at the show hall.

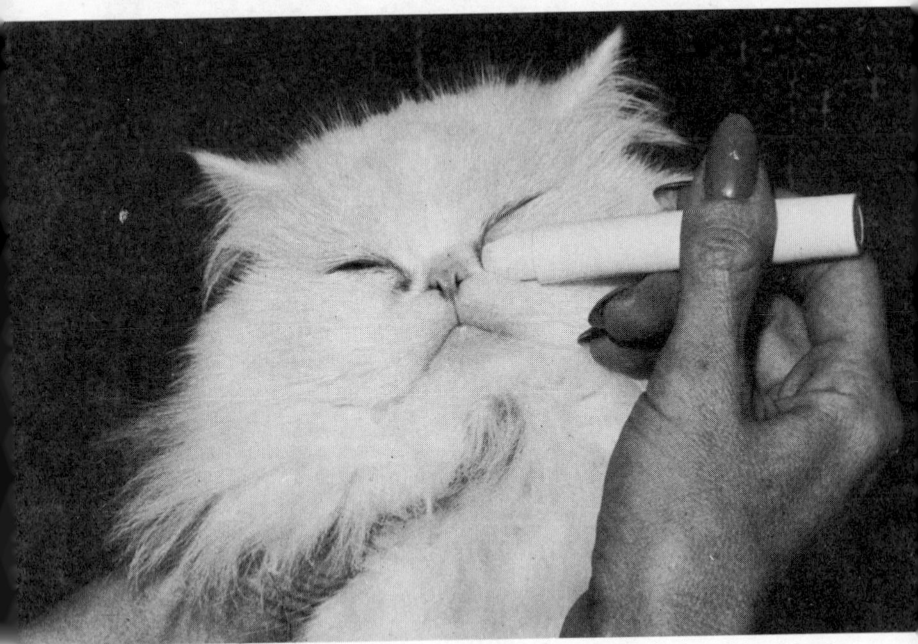

The eye is a sensitive area; when treating tear stains, don't use a chalk stick tapered to a point that is too sharp.

TEETH CARE

A cat's teeth should be clean and bright, the gums pink and healthy. Check your cat's teeth often for tartar buildup and, if necessary, take him to your vet once a year to have them scaled. Scaling teeth is an extremely tricky business requiring not only the proper equipment but also the steady experienced hand of a veterinarian. It is definitely *not* a do-it-yourself project!

The removal of dead guard hair is quite painless when properly done, but be sure the hair removed is *dead.* The removal of live hair is cause for disqualification if you want to show your cat.

A well-balanced diet with occasional crunchy kibble and large bite-size pieces of raw chunk beef will keep normal tartar formation off the teeth and provide suitable exercise for the gums as well. Unpleasant breath odors in your cat are an indication of dirty teeth, improper diet or impending illness; these signs should not be ignored.

GUARD HAIR REMOVAL

The longer, heavier and faintly darker hair which lies over the soft, fine hair of the undercoat, noticeable mainly on the back and sides is the guard hair. Sometimes during the off-season, if the cat has not been clipped down, a few old guard hairs remain to mar the new coat. These dead guard hairs look dull, dry, lifeless and darker than the new guard hair coat. The removal of *dead* guard hair and the occasional coarse white hair is called "plucking" and is considered good grooming. The removal of *live* guard hair or any off-color patches would be considered a deliberate attempt to deceive the judges and make the cat subject to disqualification. The experienced cat show judge is immediately aware of the missing live guard hair *and* the fact that the owner plucked it in an attempt to lighten the coat or make it appear more uniform in color. As you can see, grooming your pet cat is a little different than grooming your show cat.

Removal of *dead* guard hair is simple and quite painless when properly done. A few dead hairs are grasped between thumb and forefinger and pulled quickly with a wrist-snap action in the direction the coat grows till all are removed. They will come out easily with no pull or tweak to the sensitive skin.

To remove the offending whisker (broken or off-color), it can be either plucked or trimmed.

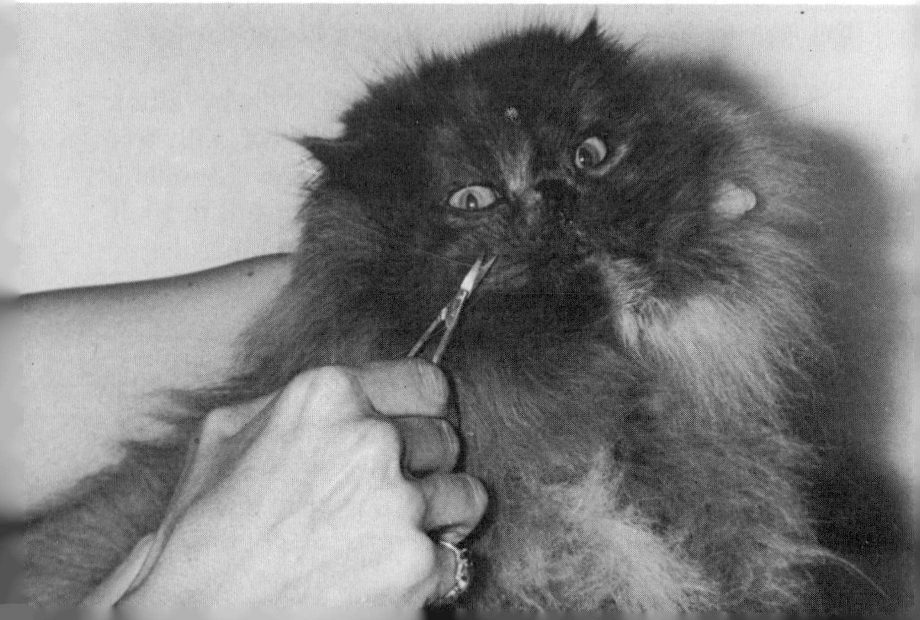

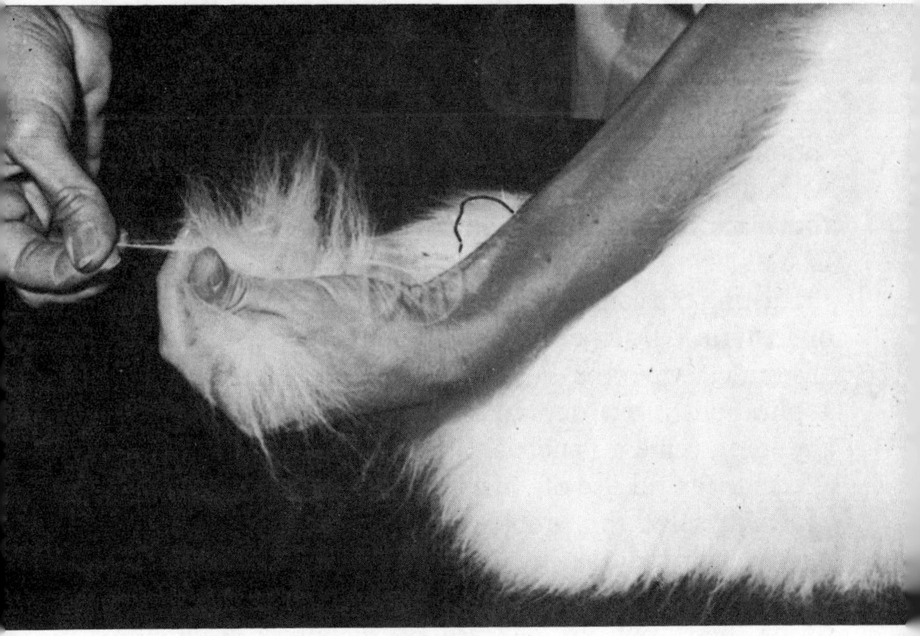

Tipping the tail hair to enhance the natural appearance.

PROBLEM WHISKER REMOVAL

The cat's whiskers create the smallest grooming problem of all. Kitty keeps her long whiskers spotless and sleek. Only the rare broken stub or the occasional white whisker on a colored cat need be removed. Tuck kitty securely beneath your left arm and hold her head gently motionless in your left hand, then quickly pluck the offending whisker in the direction of its natural growth.

COAT RUSTING

Rusting is the rusty-red discoloration of the hair caused by licking, over-exposure to direct sunlight, dampness and certain food stains. It occurs mostly in blacks, smokes and blue longhairs and is found primarily on the bib, ruff and back of the cat. Discoloration of the cream coat from similar causes is usually referred to as a "hot" or darkened coat. Black kittens are, perhaps, the most susceptible of all to the rusty coat from over-attentive mothers who never seem to quit bathing them. It is not a permanent condition, and the new coat will come in at its normal time without a sign of rust, but this is scarcely reassuring to the black kitten owner who is eager to show in Kitten Classes.

Rusting can sometimes be eased by repeated applications of Listerine. Dampen a cotton ball lightly with undiluted Listerine, wipe the rusted areas, and let dry. Several applications a few days apart are usually required before any improvement is noted. If only the tips of the hair are affected, careful use of emery cloth just prior to the show date will solve the problem. Hold the ends of the discolored hair between two pieces of *very fine* emery cloth and rub gently back and forth. Preventive measures are always best, but in the case of rusting, prevention is easier said than done.

DRY HAIR CONDITIONING

Hair that breaks too easily can often be helped with the use of a good protein coat conditioner. Cats shown at the first or last of the show season may not have their full show coats, and the length of coat and time of year is taken into consideration by the judge. A short coat on a Persian in mid-season is assumed to be the result of one of two things—either the cat has a naturally short coat, a fault for the show cat, or it is in poor condition, with hair that is brittle and breaks off short. Whatever the time of year or the natural length of the coat, a showcat's coat *must* appear robustly healthy and resilient. A dull, dry and lifeless coat on any cat prevents proper growth. If the skin seems healthy but the coat a bit dry, try one of the protein coat conditioners made especially for cats. Dry, flaky skin or rough, scaly skin, with the possible accompanying loss of hair, should prompt the owner to seek the professional advice of a licensed veterinarian. Coat conditioners can do only so much, and with their use should come the simultaneous search for the fundamental cause of the condition, which can be an inadequate diet, over-bathing that removes natural oils or undetermined illness.

POWDER PACKING

Pre-show powder packing is a decidedly messy but effective method of preparing the coat for show. After having bathed the cat on its prescribed pre-show date and thoroughly drying and combing it free of tangles, every square inch of kitty must now be packed with powder. (We suggest doing it in the cattery, the garage or some easy-to-clean room of the house . . . with the door closed!) Open the coat with a comb every inch or so, shaking powder *generously* into the hair, methodically covering

Pointed hairs around the ear line can be either broken off with the fingers or trimmed with manicure scissors.

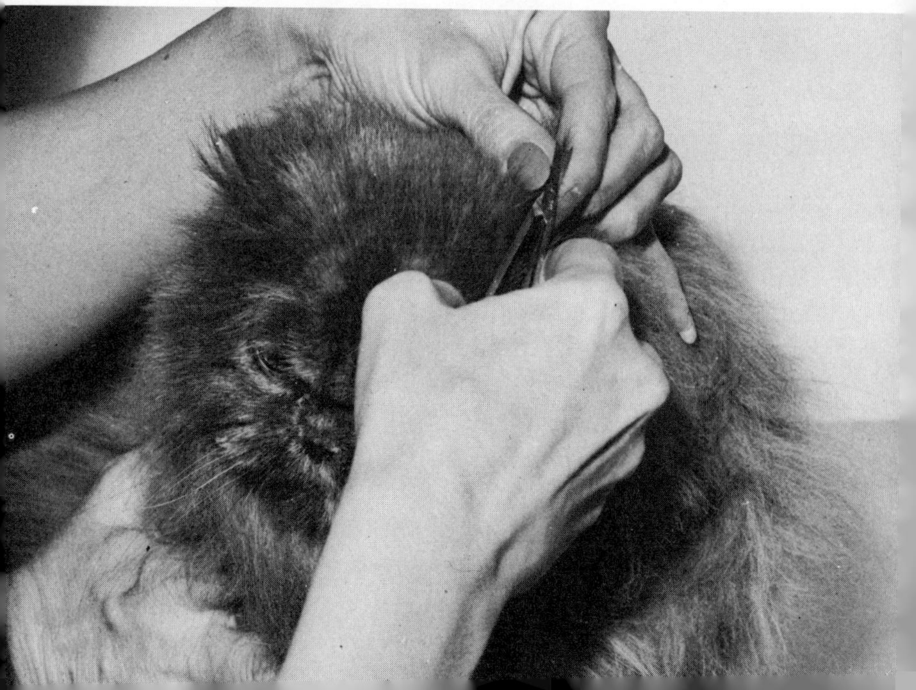

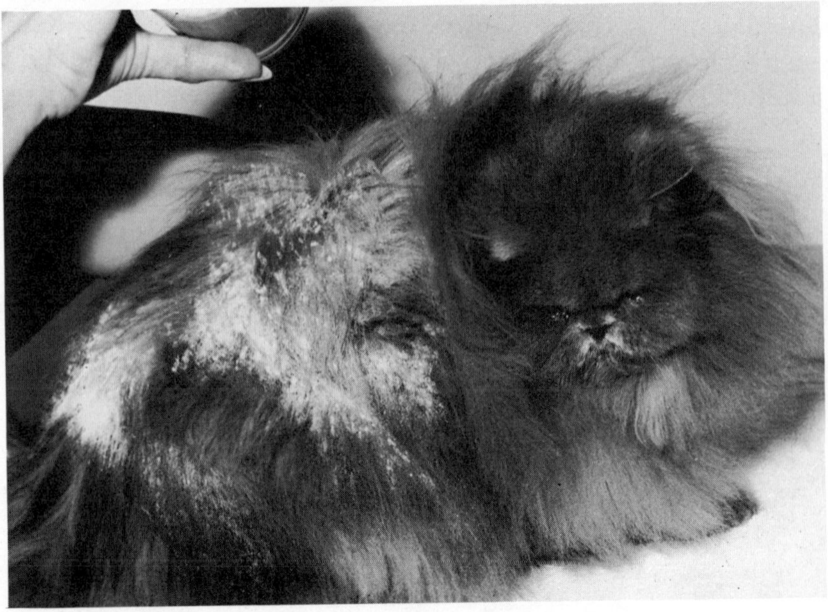

To powder kitty's back, separate the coat into inch sections while generously pouring powder into each section.

every inch of your cat, head to toe, feet, legs and tail. Comb the powder deep into the body coat, shake it into the tail, scrub it vigorously into the short hair of the legs with a soft round shoe brush, and saturate the soft underhair of the stomach and between the legs. A soft toothbrush can be used to scrub powder into the short face hair, forehead, cheeks, chin and around the ears. You will be covered with powder, but then so will the cat, and that's the important thing!

Powder-packing is essential to white, cream, blue, blue-cream, silver and cameo show cats. Smokes and Himalayans may be carefully powdered under special circumstances. Black cats are *never* powdered; the unavoidable residue of light powder would be impo[illegible] remove and would blur the shiny richness of the jet black coat. Blacks must rely on the shine of a healthy coat, a touch of coat conditioner and Fluff spray to give added body where needed.

Powder-packed show cats are usually confined to a single room or a cattery cage during this pre-show period. The powder-packing operation is repeated in full *every other day* until show time. The day before the show, *all* this powder must be either combed out or blown out of the coat with a hand-held hair dryer.

Several good grooming powders made specifically for cats are available at pet shops. While powder-packing is confined to the post-bath/pre-show time period, year-round basic grooming requires the use of once-a-week light powdering before combing to prevent mats and to keep the coat dry, fluffy light and free of excess oil. Always shield the eyes when spraying or powdering the coat.

To powder the tummy, lay the cat on her back and follow the same procedure as when powdering the back.

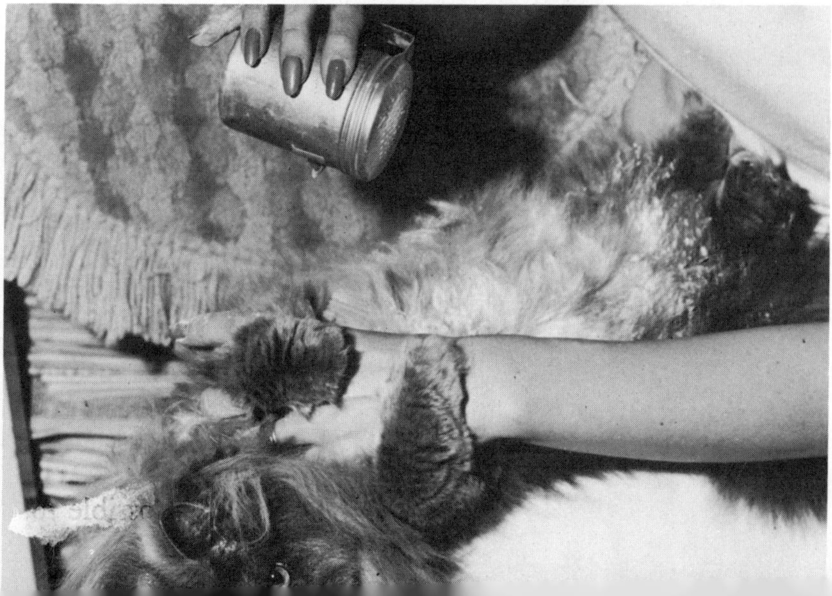

Septuple Gr. Ch. Coppertone The Wild One of Nile. From "House of Abyssinian," Maureen Nottingham, Sunland, Calif., owner.

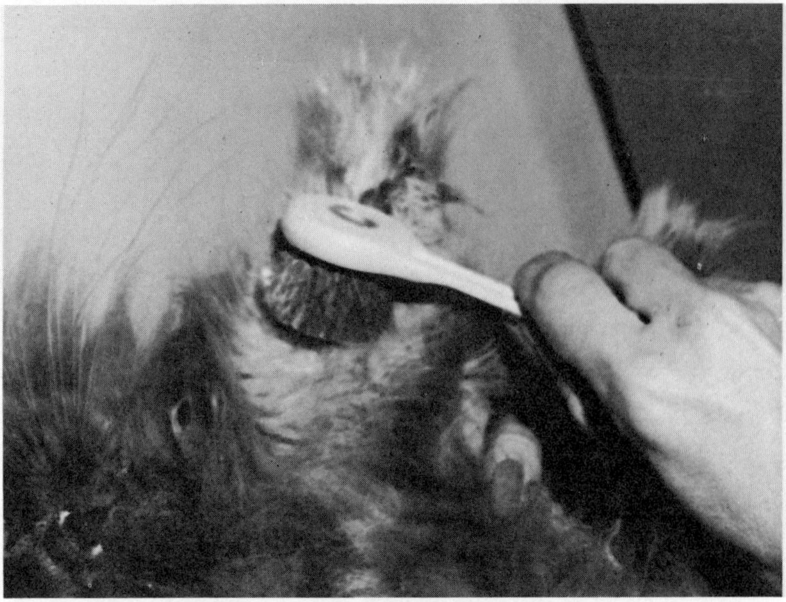

To give the short fine leg hair a fluffier look, powder the legs generously and scrub with a soft shoe brush dipped in powder.

Comb the leg hair upward, around and between the legs.

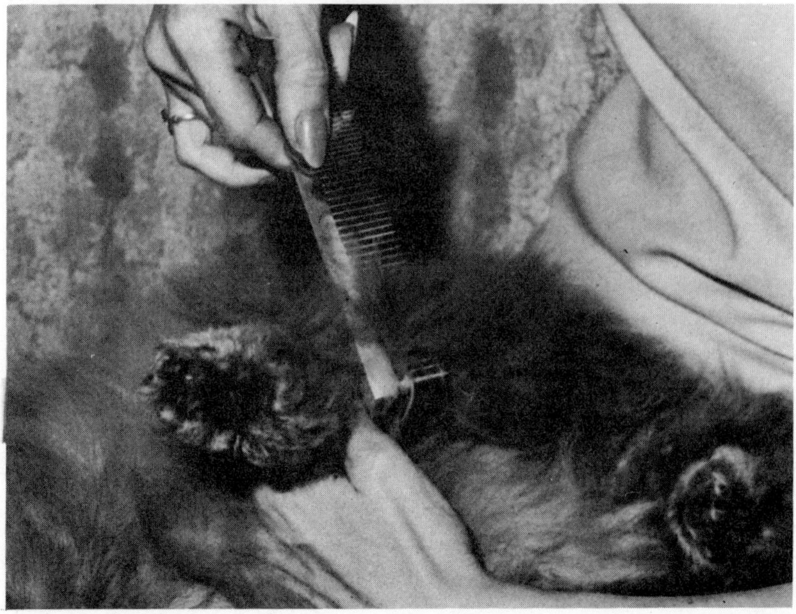

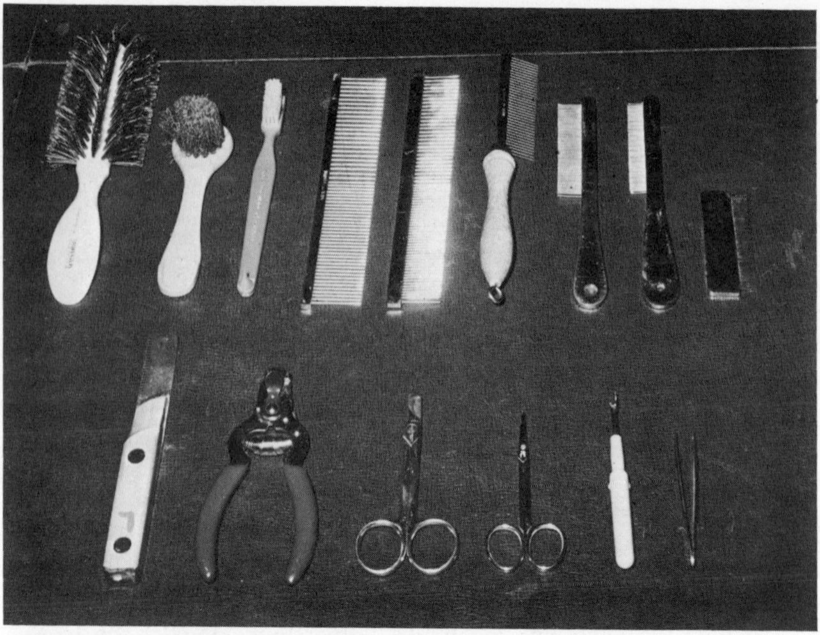

The longhair grooming kit should include combs; a pure bristle brush; seam ripper; tweezers; tooth and shoe brushes; small manicure scissors and a nail clipper.

LONGHAIR COMBS

Perhaps the single most important item in your show cat's grooming kit is the comb. The best combs for the longhair show cat are made in Belgium, England and France. Look for the name of the country stamped into the metal of the comb itself. Imported combs have longer individually set-in, pointed teeth, not dull and rounded as are the cheaper local products. Shorthair cat breeders, on the other hand, prefer combs of American origin whose blunt, round teeth cannot bruise the sensitive skin and darken the coat. The longhair cat should be equipped with three basic grooming combs: (1) an extra fine comb for face hair; (2) a fine comb for ruff, legs and feet; and (3) a medium comb for back, sides and undersides. *Never use an extremely fine comb, such as a flea comb, to groom a longhair cat*. The soft undercoat will be pulled out and leave the normally fluffy cat with a faulty close-to-the-skin look.

Clean your combs well between each use to remove any trace of natural skin oils picked up from the skin. Use mild soap, hot water and a stiff nail brush, and scrub with a vengeance. Labco Dry Cleaner may be used at the show when washing facilities are not convenient. Wash combs between each grooming of the same animal and between uses on different animals. The hair should be fabulously light and fluffy as a result of the previous ten days of powder-packing . . . *but* if the least trace of oil remains on the comb, the show coat will suffer noticeably.

COMBING PROCEDURE

Begin combing the focal point, the face, with an extra fine comb. The cheeks are combed forward and full. The top head and forehead are combed forward and down. The chin is combed up toward the nose. Ear tufts are combed out and over the ear. (A touch of powder, perhaps, to dry and separate the long tufts.) With the same comb, separate and pull the long toe tufts up between kitty's toes.

Switch to your *fine* comb and groom the legs with a firm upward motion. Leg hair is short and fine and has a tendency to cling flat to the leg. Here is where your powder-packing really pays off. If necessary, repeat the scrubbing motion on the legs with a small shoe brush dipped lightly in powder, then blow the powder away. Comb the leg hairs upward, around, and between the legs.

A *medium* comb is used on the body and most of the ruff. The bib—the area directly beneath the chin which might be covered by a small baby's bib, and sometimes is!—is combed upward and under the chin. The hair is lifted up and out with a slightly reverse motion of the wrist. Working section by section, reach deep into the coat down the length of the back and down both sides toward the tail. Very lightly groom the hair over the stud tail area. Comb the pants hair with long gentle strokes, lifting upward and outward. Holding the tip of the tail between thumb and forefinger, lift it high in the air and shake it out full. Finish by repeatedly combing the ruff upward toward the face and up and over the ears. The fine hair at the base of the ears may require the very fine comb.

A thought might cross the novice's mind. All the hairs seem to be lifted "up," never combed in the direction of their natural lie. The observation is astute . . . and perfectly

Use a fine comb to comb the face area and toe tufts. All face hair is combed toward the face; toe hair is combed upward.

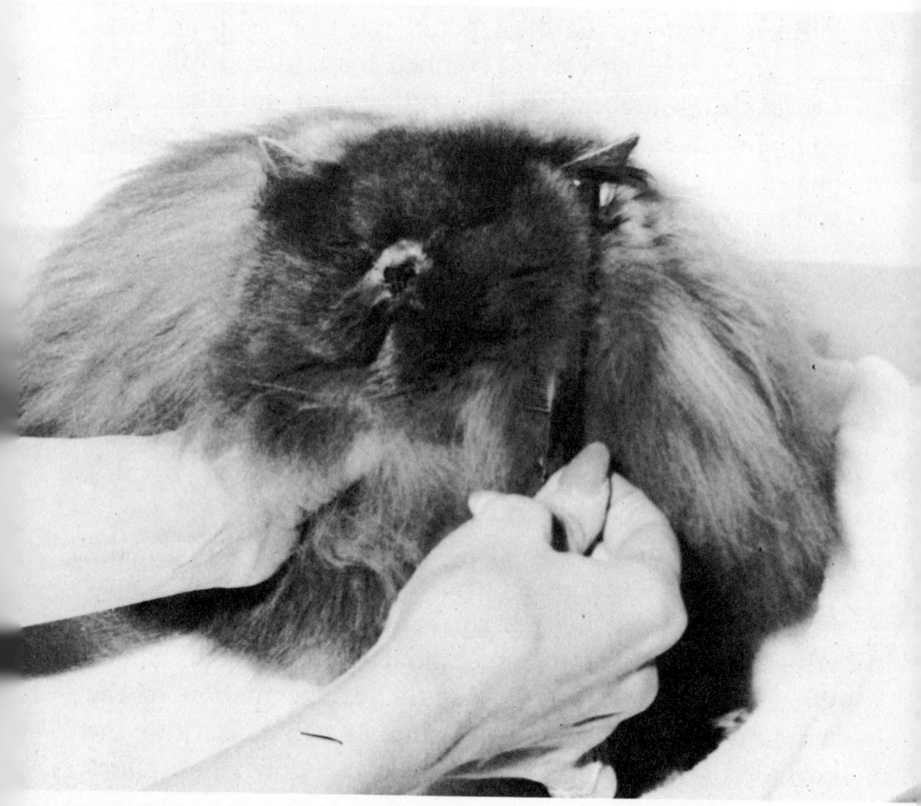

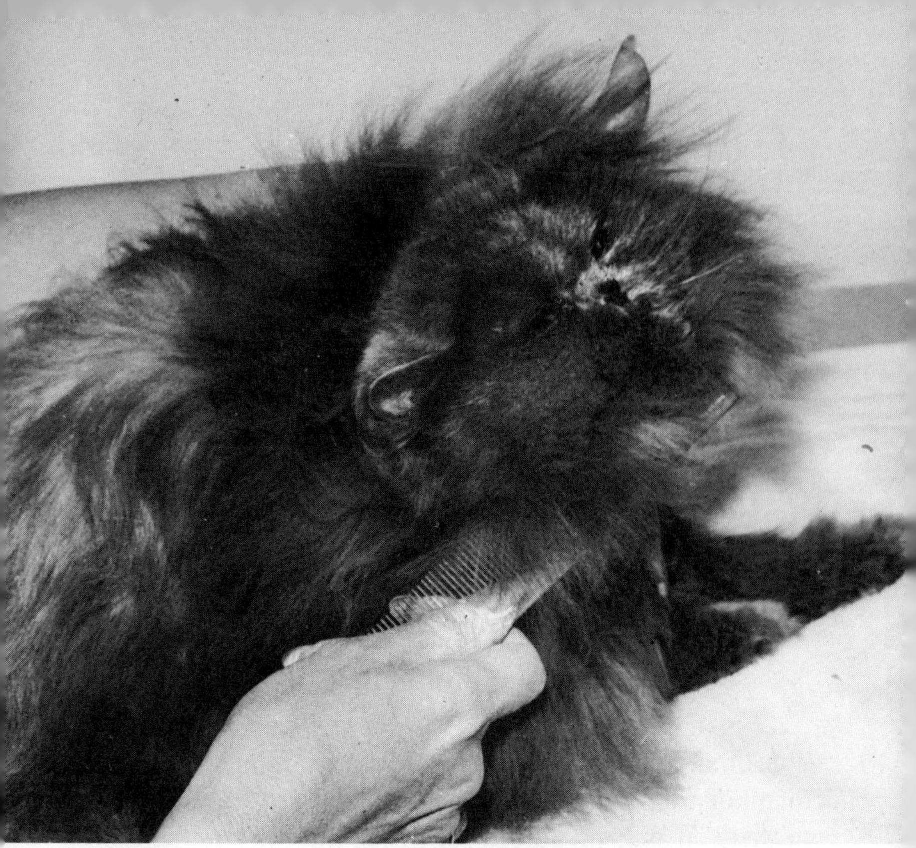

Using the fine comb, the chin hair is combed up towards the nose.

correct! To comb the full show coat—both the fine undercoat and the longer guard hair—in the direction of the natural lie would flatten its fluffy appearance. By "lifting" the coat up and slightly forward, you attain the light airy beauty desired without undue damage to the hair itself. The show coat is never forced to a reverse lie, nor is it deliberately teased or back-combed. Such action might offer a momentary effect of fluffing but would in actuality be pulling out undercoat and breaking off fragile hair in the process. Lifting the coat, on the other hand, gives the desired height safely. The tips of the long guard hair will assume the natural directional lie in the span of a few moments, while the undercoat remains in the uplift position beneath it.

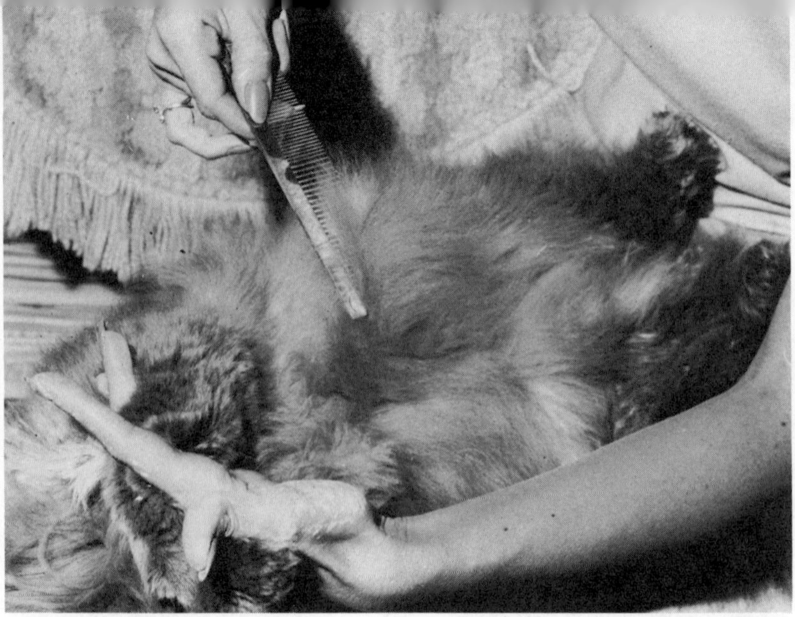

With a medium comb, the bib hair is combed toward the chin and the tummy hair against its natural lie for fullness.

A final word on the subject of combing: always remember that most cats have areas that are super-sensitive to them. It will vary from cat to cat and may be the flanks, the tail, the stomach area or between the legs. Some cats are ticklish, some are skin-sensitive and some are merely touchy. You, the all-knowing owner, must be patient, understanding and affectionate. These areas must be properly groomed, of course, but you should keep it to a minimum. Do it quickly and move on.

GROOMING THE KITTEN

Kitten grooming should begin as soon as the kitten is weaned. It consists of simple combing of the longhair kitten and gentle brushing of the shorthair kitten. Grooming, for grooming's sake, is quite unnecessary at six weeks of age and is intended only to establish a pleasant daily routine for the kitten's future adult life. Grooming of young kittens should be kept to about a minute or less at first, gradually increasing as the kitten grows older.

Twice-a-week grooming is usually sufficient for the normal show-age kitten. Seldom occurring before one year of age, problem or curly coats may require more frequent care. Be patient during these kitten grooming training sessions . . . *but be firm* . . . for the good grooming habits established in kittenhood will dominate his entire adult show life. There will be those who love it and others who merely tolerate it because it has become routine. Whatever the reason, practice makes (the kitten) perfect. Grooming procedures are basically those previously set forth in this chapter for adult cats, except that kittens are more generously powdered with patience.

The implements of grooming for shorthair kittens remain basically the same as those items specified for the longhairs, excluding only those items designed specifically for the long coat. The shorthair exhibitor substitutes soft pure bristle brushes, a chamois and silk scarves. If combs are used, they are metal combs of American origin whose blunt round teeth prevent possible bruising or discoloration of the delicate shorthair coat. A man's pocket comb is favored by many silver Tabby breeders. Basic at-home grooming procedures are far less complex for the shorthair breeder. The nails are clipped, and the ears and eyes are cleaned as instructed in this chapter. If in good health, shorthair cats have little problem with eye secretion and seldom require little more than a drop of Visine to brighten the eyes just before judging. The tail area is frequently checked for any sign of stud tail grease and, if needed, bathed with liquid detergent. NP-27 in powder form, obtainable at most drug stores in the foot care section, is particularly effective for between-bathing care of the shorthair stud tail problem. Grooming powder, if used at all, must be blown out or brushed free of the coat before the day of the show. Never use a flea *spray* preparation during show season. The shorthair coat will immediately take on a tacky oily appearance which nothing short of a fresh bath will repair.

Gentle brushing comprises the major part of the shorthair's grooming session. Use light brush strokes from shoulder to rump, from neck down the tummy and between the legs, always moving with the natural lay of the hair. Vigorous brushing or the use of stiff-bristled brushes will bruise the sensitive skin and darken the coat for the remainder of the season. For this reason, many breeders stroke their lovely shorthairs only with their hands.

THE NIGHT BEFORE THE SHOW

The night before the show is the time for last minute chores and a quick reappraisal of a job well done. Claws must be freshly clipped, the ears and tail tipped. To avoid that lynx-like look to an otherwise perfect ear set, the small point of hair which stands up above the natural round ear line may be broken off with the fingers or *carefully* trimmed with manicure scissors to conform with the true line of the ear. Never touch the hair that grows in or around the other part of the ears except to clean or comb it. Give the tail a similar treatment, but this time break the tips to avoid a false pointed look to an otherwise full, fluffy tail.

Kitty is ready for the cat show. Suddenly you look at her with a new sense of values. Can this lovely animal be yours? It's like watching a tomboy daughter blossom overnight into Prom Queen. Kitty has become the beautiful princess of a feline fairy tale, transformed from a mischievous kitten imp into a beauty queen. Bring on the competition . . . how could the judges resist! But that's tomorrow . . . tonight it's a good dinner and early to bed for both you and Miss Feline Fancypants. The next two days will be full and exciting.

3

BATHING THE LONGHAIRED CAT

A pretty girl would not enter a beauty contest without bathing first, nor would the experienced exhibitor present a dirty cat to the judges. An all-over bath, however, should be given only when the cat is dirty enough or the coat oily enough to warrant it. Frequent unnecessary bathing will dry the fragile show coat and cause it to look dull and lifeless. Excessive bathing will also remove the natural skin oils which protect the animal against fungus and related dry skin problems.

Too many cooks may spoil the broth, but two people are far better than one when it comes to bathing a cat. The stand-by can hand you equipment when your hands are full of wet-and-wiggly feline, answer the phone, and reject door-to-door salesmen. It is difficult, no, *impossible* to leave a sopping wet cat alone in the sink even for a moment.

BATHING EQUIPMENT

Assemble all the equipment you will need for kitty's bath in advance. A sample sinktop display might include: three large bath towels; a wash cloth; cat shampoo; liquid detergent; cream rinse (pre mixed, if required); a soft toothbrush; an extra cup or plastic glass; comb; cotton and a small cage or carrier for confining the cat while drying. There are many brands of pet shampoo on the market, available in a variety of show coat colors and an even

Commercial shampoo products like the one shown here are made especially for use on cats and are available at pet shops and other outlets specializing in animal care products.

greater variety of prices. One of the safest and best shampoos for cats and kittens is Lambert-Kay's Tearless Protein Shampoo for Cats. They will not sting the eyes or dry the coat, yet do remove normal oil and dirt with simple bathing. Lambert-Kay makes a particularly good blue shampoo for brightening white coats. Any very mild soap or non-pet shampoo can be used, but place one drop of mineral oil in each eye before proceeding with the bath to safeguard against eye irritation.

BEFORE-BATH PROCEDURES

Prepare your cat for its bath by clipping its claws, removing all mats and combing out all loose or dead hair. Then *very gently* press a small bit of cotton in each ear to keep out the water. Care should be taken that the cotton remains in the outer ear area. Kitty is now ready for the bath.

WHERE TO BATHE

If at all possible, use a waist-high sink that has a spray hose or spray attachment. In lieu of a spray unit, fill the sink with *tepid* water to the cat's chest level and use a plastic cup or glass to pour water over the animal. The spray attachment is far superior in that it penetrates the thick coat clear to the skin and removes all traces of dirt and soap residues which may dull the show coat. Place the cat in the sink on a rubber mat with holes in it. The security of a solid gripping surface will make the chore of bathing much easier than setting the animal directly on the slippery porcelain surface of the sink.

BATHING PROCEDURE

Begin bathing the head by filling a plastic cup with tepid water and pouring it slowly over the cat's head to dampen it. Pouring is far less frightening than the spray in

To wet the coat for bath, gently pour water over the cat's head. This method is less frightening than a spray in the face.

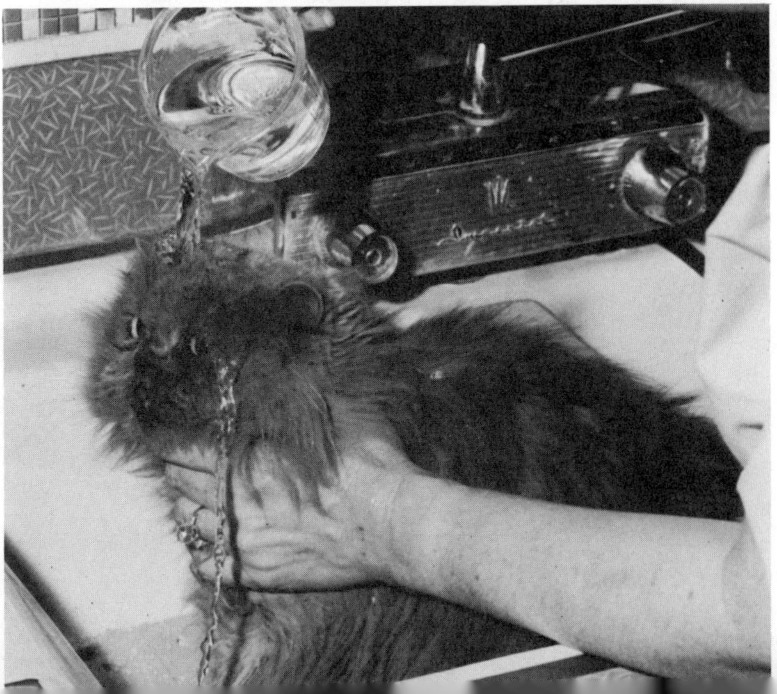

his face. Shampoo the head first; then, using the wash cloth in the ears and around the eyes, gradually work beneath the chin and down the neck. Leaving the shampoo suds in the coat, work your way over the shoulders, down the back, between the legs and finally soaping the tummy. Work up a good thick lather and massage it well into the coat. Leaving the lather in the coat, place the cat's tail on the drainboard's edge and pour a mild dish detergent (green Palmolive dish detergent recommended) over the full length of the tail. *Gently* scrub down to the skin with a soft toothbrush where the oily secretion is the worst. This is especially important for males with a greasy stud tail problem. Do *not* use detergent on any other part of the cat's body!

Rinse all shampoo thoroughly out of the coat. Rinse until you are sure it is all out, then to be safe rinse another full minute! If you have used a sinkful of water rather than a spray attachment, empty the soapy water before the rinse cycle. Empty again for a second clean-water rinse.

Use a facecloth around the face to work the lather into the coat.

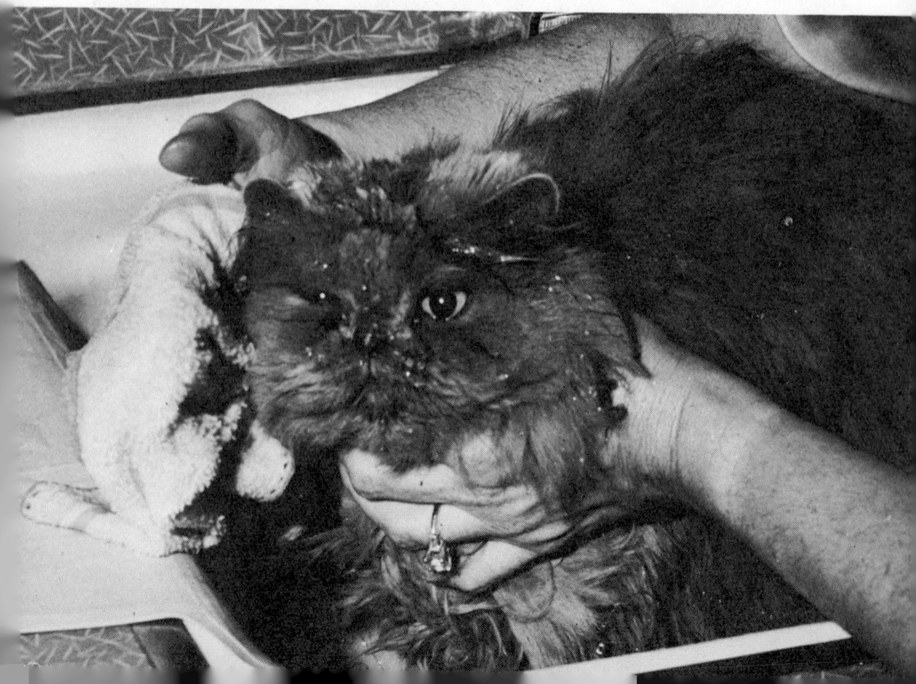

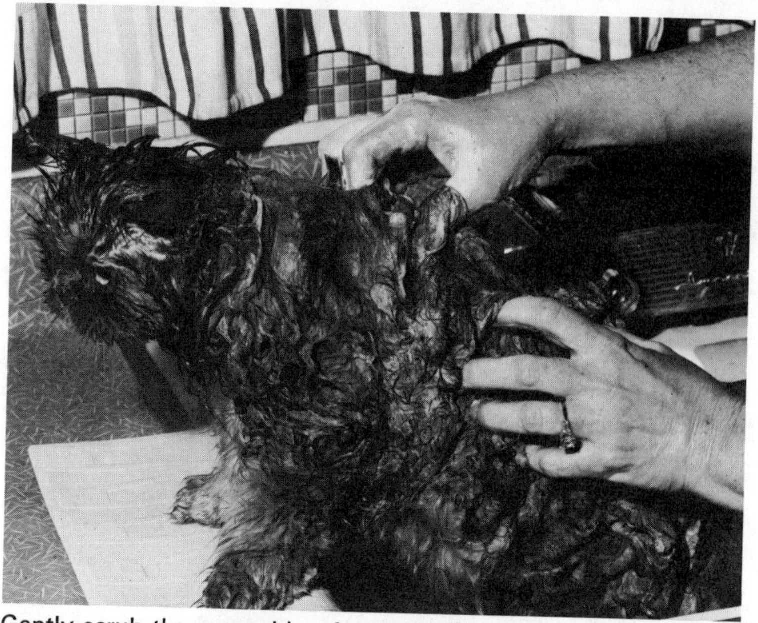

Gently scrub the ears with a facecloth. To prevent water or soap from dripping into the ear canal, use cotton plugs.

Massage the shampoo into the coat with the fingertips, working from the nape down to the base of the tail and from the tummy around and down the legs.

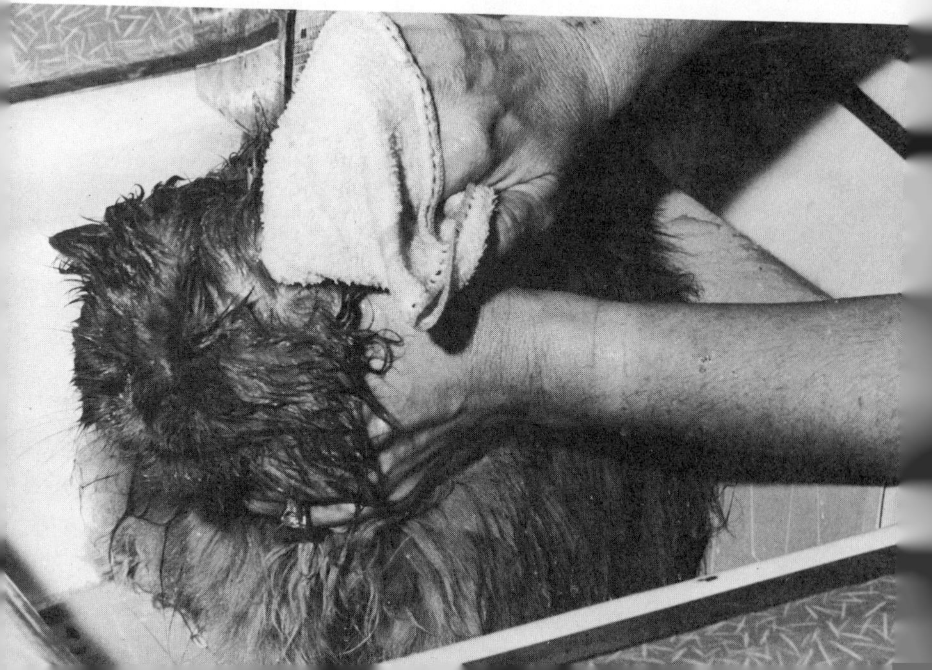

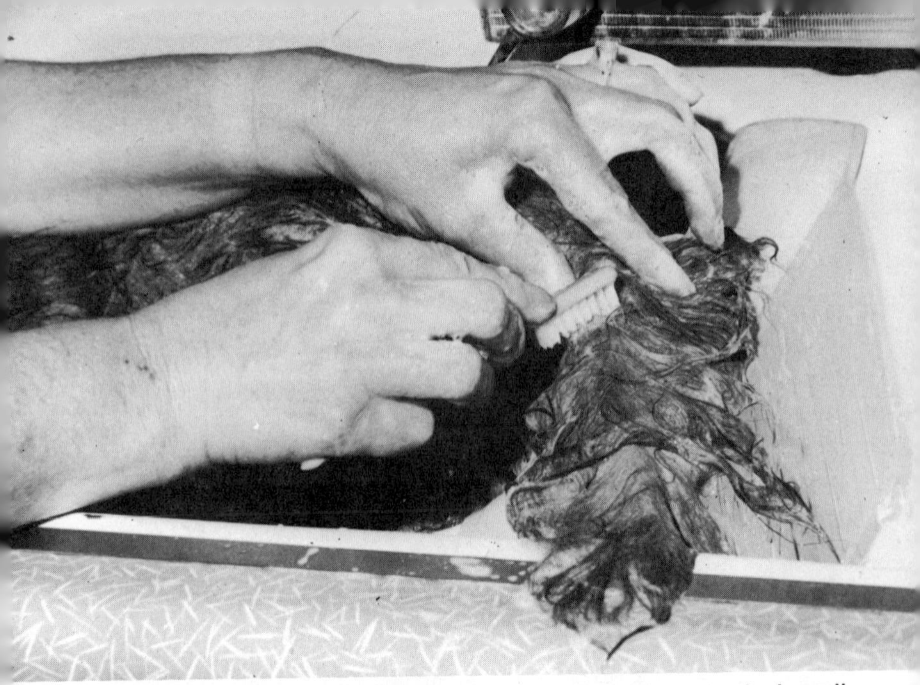

Use a mild dish detergent and a soft toothbrush to wash the tail deep down into the skin where the oily secretion is the worst.

Rinse *twice* and be sure to remove any trace of soap that may film the coat. If a cream rinse is used, rinse well so that it will not leave an oily base.

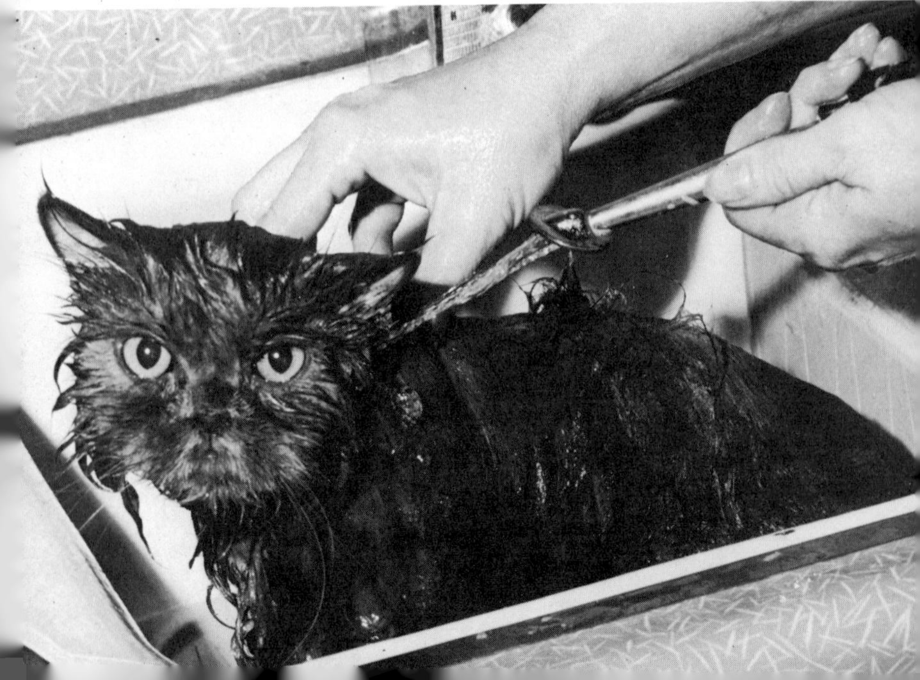

Nothing dulls a coat more than a careless soapy residue. Use a cream rinse, if desired, working it thoroughly into the clean shining coat, then rinse again. Remember, cream rinse will help eliminate tangles in a long coat, but it also leaves less body to the coat.

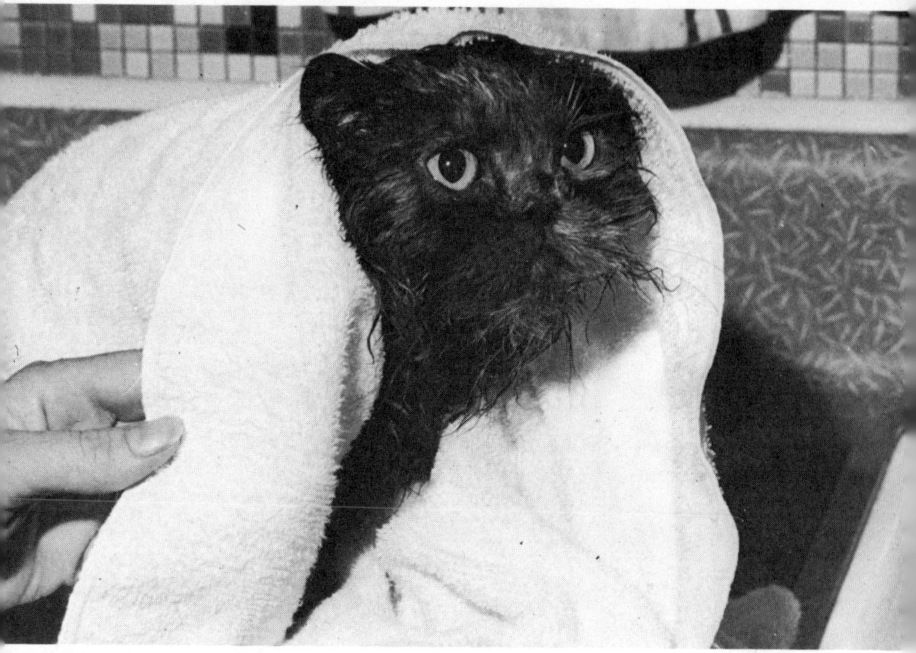

Wrap kitty in a towel *immediately* after bathing to prevent chill and to gently squeeze all water from the coat.

DRYING PROCEDURE

Once your cat is out of the water, work as rapidly as possible to prevent chill. Remove the cotton from the ears and wipe her face with the towel. Then gently squeeze the excess water out of the coat, by working from top to tummy, between and down the legs. Put the wet towel aside and take a fresh dry one. Towel-dry the long coat, taking great care not to tangle the coat. A third towel should be placed in the bottom of the drying cage or carrier. Place the carrier in a warm draft-free location and use a blower

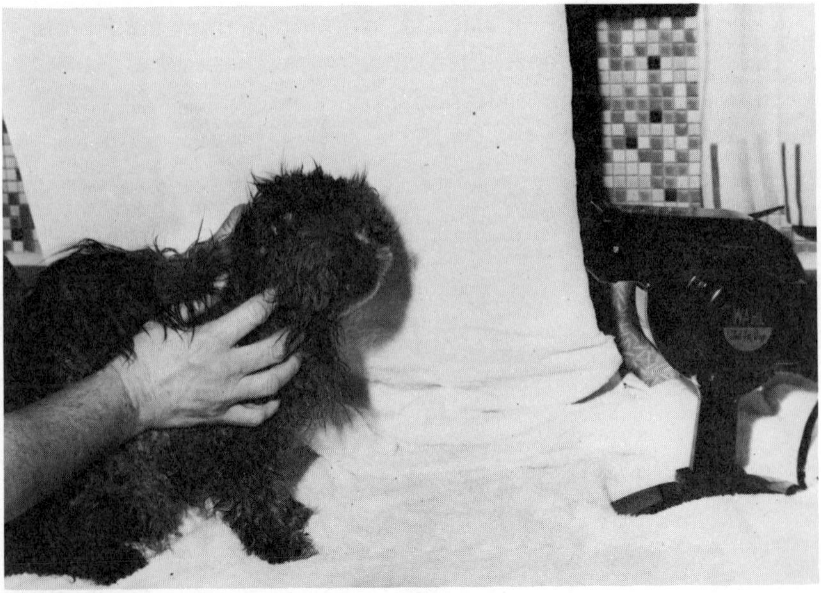

Hold the cat firmly while drying. *Never* overheat the cat.

Use a comb to speed the drying cycle, untangle the hair and fluff the coat.

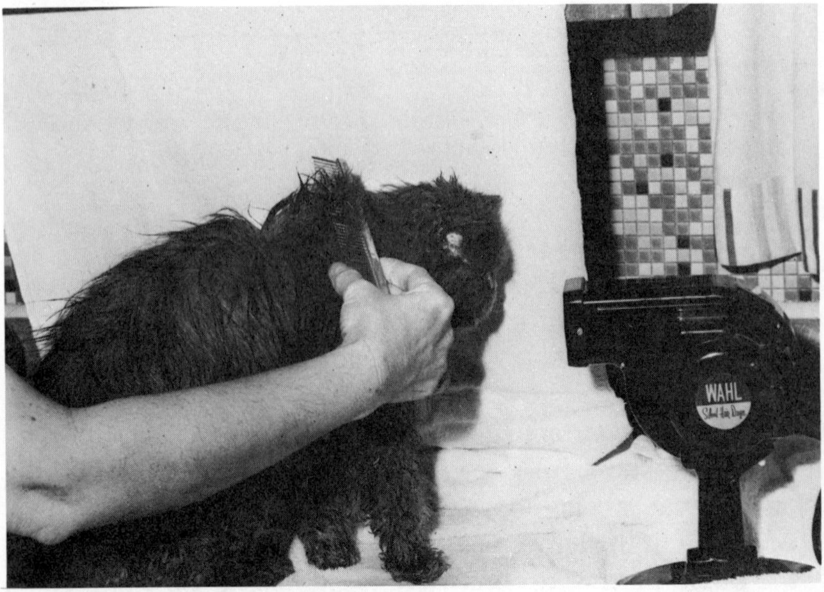

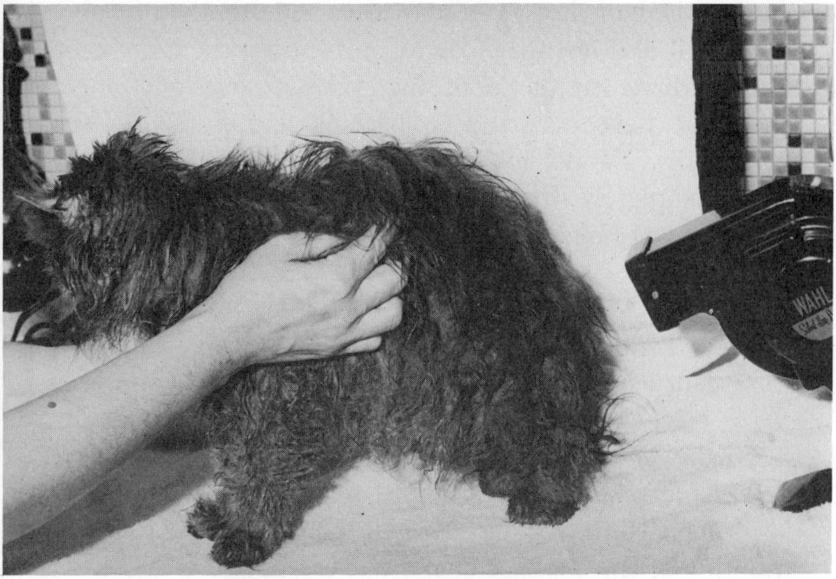

An adjustable hairdryer directs warm air where needed.

Fresh as a feline daisy . . . now where's my treat?

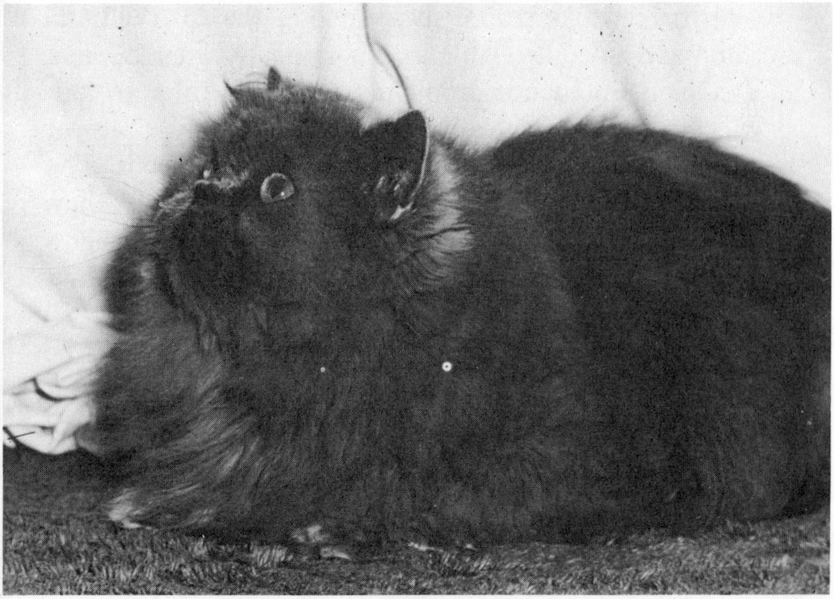

hair dryer with a *reliable* heat control. Do not overheat the cat! As the hair dries, you may use a wide-toothed comb to gently lift and open the coat. Comb-lifting the hair before a warm dryer speeds the drying cycle, removes any tangles that may have occurred in bathing and fluffs the coat beautifully. Do not allow the cat to roam the house until he is completely dry. Damp hair attracts dust, dirt and a multitude of housekeeping sins.

WHEN TO BATHE FOR SHOW

The "right time" to bathe a show cat is almost as important as "how" to bathe it. The time varies between three days to three weeks before the show, depending upon the breed and the color and texture of its coat. It also depends upon the cat and her individual ability to keep herself immaculate between the time of the bath and the time of the show. Generally speaking, very fine coats, such as are found on kittens and silvers, should be bathed at least a week and preferably a week-and-a-half before the show. A few rare exceptions must be bathed as long as two to three weeks before show time or the coat will still be limp and uncontrollable in grooming. Whites, because of a color maintenance problem, are bathed three to four days before show dates. Cats with very oily coats or persistent stud tail secretion are bathed four to six days prior to public appearance. The average longhair show cat, however, is usually bathed a week before the show and hopefully kept out from under the bed until show time.

Bathing is an experience most cats do not relish, so be kind, patient and understanding if she is frightened or disagreeable. She will forgive you . . . a pleasant treat of your cat's favorite food will help restore you to good graces faster than you can say *cat*astrophe!

4

SPECIAL COLORS, SPECIAL CARE

Grooming procedures are basically the same for all longhair cats. Special colors, however, present problems which require special attention. Common sense tells the novice that he must not sprinkle white powder on a black cat, but it does not always offer a logical substitute in its stead. Unfortunately, there is no magician's magic hat from which to pull miracles, but there are certain small tricks of the trade which should be passed along to the novice. Many of these special care suggestions have been grouped by cat color as a convenient reminder for the novice who already has "too many details" to remember.

WHITE PERSIANS

The most important thing about showing a white cat is to have him sparkling *white* white. Tattletale gray is no more popular at the cat show than on your clothesline. Always bathe the white cat with a good brand of blue shampoo. Since the white coat stains and discolors more noticeably than colored coats, care should be taken to avoid dampness, food, urine and saliva stains. Stubborn yellow stains may require spot saturation with hydrogen peroxide (3% solution) on a piece of cotton. Pack the cleansed area with cornstarch while still damp, dry thoroughly, then comb out. Repeat, if needed. Do not permit the peroxide solution to get into the eyes, ears, nose or mouth.

Grand Ch. La Cresta's White Robin, white Persian female; breeder Betty Meins; owner Pam Prokop.

White Persians show eye stains more readily than cats of other colors. Warm-water washing of the area followed by a cornstarch pack will remove normal tear stains. Stubborn tear lines may require the use of an eye stain remover. Follow directions explicitly, dry thoroughly, and if necessary use a little white chalk stick over the stain area for daily care or during touch-up grooming at the show hall.

White cats should always be powder-packed well in advance of the show; the powder-packing should be repeated every other day from bath time to show time. Blow *all* powder out of the coat before presenting your showpiece to the judge. Remember, use white terry towels or white paper towels for kitty's carrier, and use litter or white paper towels for the sanitary pan to prevent foot pad stain.

White Robin resting between shows on her feathery throne.

BLACK PERSIANS

Good sound black color is very difficult to obtain. Crossbreeding with blues for type or coat improvement often results in a faulty blue-gray undercoat. Black Persians should be jet-black to the skin. The color problem is further complicated by their unfortunate tendency to rust. Avoid over-exposure to direct sunlight whenever possible. Do not allow the black show cat to "catnap" in the window or on the carpet in front of the glass doors that let in the sun. Avoid dampness wherever possible, and don't allow playing in the bathtub or sleeping in the wash basin. Once rusting has occurred, there is no miracle cure. Try repeated applications of Listerine and the careful use of a very fine emery cloth on the tips of the hair.

Do not powder black cats! Bathe at least two weeks before the show to allow the body and natural sheen to return to the coat. Three to four days before the show, try a *little* Shaklee's, St. Aubrey's or Dramoricide coat conditioners. After rubbing some on the hands, work into the coat for added body and luster. At the show, judicious use of coat conditioner or Listerine adds last-minute shine. Don't overdo it! Fluff spray should be used sparingly. Wipe the coat lightly and carefully with a *silk* scarf or velvet mitten to remove any dust, lint or accidental powder residue that might smudge the rich dark coat.

The familiar dandruff problem in black Persians can be the result of many contributing factors, among which are the lack of vitamins, a poor diet or dry skin. Try improving the diet by adding more raw meat and vitamin/mineral supplements. A change of shampoos may help. Try a top quality protein shampoo and protein rinse made especially for cats. Yeast powder or tablets are believed by many breeders of blacks to improve coat condition and intensify the deep black color. If the dandruff condition continues, consult your veterinarian.

Africat's Jungle Genii, black Persian female; breeder-owner Wanita Floyd.

BLUE PERSIANS

Blues have unusually deep, heavy coats which seldom lack body or length. Powder-packing is a must for the blue coat before every show. (Weekly off-season powdering is suggested to keep the long coat mat free.) Daily combing is usually required for show quality blues and is recommended for pet type blues. An occasional blue Persian may have what is termed a "curly" coat which no amount of grooming will cure. Powder the curly areas frequently. The last second before presentation to the judge, comb the tummy and any other curly area and try not to maul it while carrying kitty from grooming table to judging cage.

Peroxide solutions *should never* be used on blues or any other colored coat. Food or urine stains require immediate spot cleaning with mild soap or shampoo and warm water. Try Labco for stubborn stains. Rusting may be treated with Listerine, as with the black coat.

BLUE-CREAM PERSIANS

Blue-creams have few problems with coat body or length. They should be treated as the blue coat combing to advantage so cream patching will show.

CREAM PERSIANS

Cream Persian coats are similar in type, length and body to the blue coat and should be treated in a similar manner. Avoid over-exposure to direct sunlight, which will redden or darken the desirable light cream coat. Avoid contact with dampness, which will cause a rusting effect. Do *not* use newsprint in the cream Persian's carrier or litter pan. Use white terrycloth, white paper towels or litter to prevent foot pad stains.

Tear stains show up on the pale cream coat and will darken the tear lines permanently if not cared for properly. Treat as aforementioned with warm water or eye stain remover and cornstarch packing and drying.

Quad. Ch. Zoda Candace of La Cresta, blue Persian female; breeder Mrs. Zoe R. McEachern; owner Betty Meins.

Dbl. Gr. Ch. Zoda Rose Parade of La Cresta, cream Persian male, at the age of seven months; breeder Mrs. Zoe R. McEachern, owner Betty Meins.

SILVER PERSIANS

Silver Persians have long, fragile coats. The hair is extremely fine in texture and very perishable. The undercoat tangles easily and combs out in chunks if handled roughly. Lacking body, the silver coat must be washed well in advance of show dates with a shampoo made expressly for silvers or, lacking that, for whites. Yellow stains are treated with hydrogen peroxide (3% solution) on cotton, as mentioned under white Persians, followed by cornstarch packing and a thorough drying and combing out.

Special attention should be paid to eye stains. Cleanse regularly and do not allow the tear stain line to become a permanent stain. Since silvers have an especially long, flowing ruff, care should be taken to avoid food stains during show season.

Silvers *must* be powder-packed, and extreme care should be taken in combing the ruff or frill to avoid damage or breakage of the fragile hair. Judicious use of Fluff spray is recommended at the show.

Grand Ch. Charlwood's Prima Donna, silver Persian female; breeder owner Ruth Dresser Pierce.

BLACK SMOKE PERSIANS

Smoke Persians are in full show coat only about three months out of the year and are difficult for the novice to exhibit. The long coat and regal white ruff do not appear until December or January and disappear suddenly toward the end of March. Good coat color is hard to obtain. The undercoat must be a sparkling white and the long outer coat a rich jet black. The "perfect" smoke coat will appear black, except for the luxurious white ruff. Blowing gently into the black coat will reveal the white beneath.

The smoke show coat is treated basically as a black coat and should be bathed two weeks before show dates in order to regain body and luster. Smoke coats may *not* be powder-packed but should be combed frequently and *gently* to prevent knotting of the fine and fragile hair in the ruff, undersides and pants. Coat conditioners may be used sparingly for luster and body, and Fluff spray used lightly on the ruff only during touch-up grooming at the show. Use a silk scarf or velvet mitten for last-minute dust removal and added shine. The use of a white chalk stick as a grooming aid to dry and separate ear tufts and ruff is permitted *only* if the ruff is a snowy white in its original state. It is not permitted as a means of falsely lightening the color of the ruff. Rust-colored tips of the ruff, back and side hair may be carefully removed with very fine emery cloth, as instructed, or treated with Listerine.

When the smoke coat is dropped, usually about the end of March, the undercoat loses its sparkling whiteness and the ruff disappears completely. Faint tabby-like stripes may appear temporarily on the legs and tail. Do not be concerned. The smoke is not necessarily mismarked; it is just the erratic growth of the distinctive smoke coat. Many judges will take into consideration the perishable smoke coat and short season, but we feel it is highly unfair to the animal to show it at such an obvious disadvantage. Experienced smoke breeders exhibit their adult smokes at every possible show during the "full coat" period and avoid the "short coat" season except for kitten exhibition.

Grand Ch. Knollcrest's Smoke Princess, black smoke Persian female; breeder owners Carlos and Mary Noriega.

BLUE SMOKE PERSIANS

Blue smokes are powder-packed in the same manner as the blue Persian, and all traces of powder should be blown out before show time. White chalk may be used on ear tufts and ruff *only* if the frill is perfectly white and no deception is possible. Rusting is treated with Listerine and, if necessary, the use of very fine emery cloth on the tips of the hair.

TABBY PERSIANS

The most important thing to remember about grooming the tabby Persian is not to distract from the light and dark pattern of the markings. Do not lift or fluff the coat with a comb except around the face and ruff. The coat should be combed in the direction of its natural lie, showing the distinctive markings to best advantage. Silver tabby Persians may be powdered a week before the show, if desired, but it is *crucial* that any trace of powder be removed prior to show time. Red and brown tabby Persians should never be powdered and must rely on coat conditioners and gentle combing. Careful use of Listerine rubbed first on the hands, then on the pattern, twenty minutes before judging will sometimes clear a "smudgy" coat. Silk scarves or velvet mittens may be used, if needed, as with blacks and smokes.

TORTIE PERSIANS

Tortie coats are treated in much the same manner as the black coat. Allow ten days after bathing to regain coat body and luster. Comb to show patching to best advantage, but do *not* powder the tortie coat. Coat conditioner may be used several days before the show. Listerine or Fluff is used in touch-up grooming at the show.

CAMEO PERSIANS

The cameo owner should use only shampoos designed for whites or silvers. Fine-textured coats should be

Quad. Ch. Goforth's Sugar Baby of Patilla, tortie point Himalayan female; breeder Mrs. J. F. Goforth; owner Mrs. Patricia Mills.

bathed two weeks before the show, normal coats ten days prior to show time. Cameos may be powder-packed a week before the judging, if you are careful to remove every trace of powder. Comb as you would comb the smoke, fluffing the ruff, face and pants hair only. Body hair is lifted, then gently combed in the direction of its natural lie. Avoid over-exposure to direct sunlight or contact with dampness which might darken the delicate cameo coat.

HIMALAYANS

Like the lovely Siamese from which he takes his exquisite coloring, the Himalayan has extremely sensitive

Quad. Ch. Zoda Candace of La Cresta.

Zoda Lalique, Blue female kitten, sired by Zoda Gr. Ch. Mon Ami Pierrot. Dam is Wimauma LaLange of Zoda. Zoe R. McEachern, breeder. Mr. Robert Blomquist, owner.

Gr. Ch. Frosty Cu-Ling of Sai-Ban, frost point Siamese female, sired by Shanghai Pongee of Kaywin. Dam is Carlu's Holly Cho Sen. Larry Foushier, San Diego, breeder. Edward J. Bowers, Lemon Grove, Calif., owner.

skin. Any stress condition, fever, illness or injury may result in a darkened coat for the remainder of the season or until the new coat comes in. Special care must be taken in combing, grooming and even playing with the lovely Himalayan if you wish to show him.

Himalayan coats vary greatly in texture—some are long and fine like the blue, whereas others are thick and plushy. Bathing schedules must be chosen to fit your Himalayan's coat type. Very fine coats should be bathed ten days to two weeks prior to show time so they may regain body and luster; the coarser coat should be bathed perhaps only a week in advance. Himalayans may be *carefully* powder-packed at least a week before show dates, if desired, and *if* you take great care not to powder the color points or tail. Powder must be thoroughly blown from the coat before the show to prevent smudging or muddying of the color points. A little Listerine or coat conditioner during touch-up grooming at the show will remove unnoticed powder residues and brighten color points. Himalayan coats, not having the benefit of the body and texture of the blue coat, will usually benefit from the conservative use of Fluff or similar spray just before judging call.

5

PRESERVING THE SHOW COAT

Assuming you have followed the suggestions in the previous chapters, your cat is now healthy, happy and beautifully groomed. It's time to relax . . . almost. Remember, the plush show coat can look like a motheaten mink in just a few days if not properly protected! The "strictly pet" Persian may be allowed unlimited privileges at play but, unfortunately, the "show" longhairs must pay a price for their beauty.

SUPERVISED CAT-PLAY

During the show season, play time must be sensibly supervised in controlled surroundings. When longhair cats or kittens are allowed to participate in rough-and-tumble play sessions, the show coat will suffer badly. If left to their own devices, the cats will romp through the house, roll on rough carpets and wrestle under the bed, leaving a well-marked trail of hair behind them. In the name of jolly good fun, hair is pulled out or broken off, and the magnificent coat that took months to grow is suddenly destroyed. Instead of rough cat playing some cats lick more than others and perhaps some of it is done out of boredom. Always provide your cat with enough safe non-abrasive toys to keep him occupied, changing them from time to time. The show coat of the longhair cat is a very fragile commodity and one that cannot be repaired or replaced until next season. Treat it gently.

Cat tree carpeting and toys should be smooth and non-abrasive to avoid coat damage.

SUPERVISED SURROUNDINGS

If your show cats are confined at any time, make certain that the walls and floors of the cages are smooth and free from abrasive surfaces. Splintered wood can snag the long show coat and leave it a patchwork of disaster, and rough wooden floors can pull the long tufts of hair from the feet. Wire caging must be free from broken strands, with rough ends completely concealed. The show cat who paces should never be confined, because the constant brushing against wire or walls can completely destroy the show coat on one side. Avoid old wire or nails with rust spots to discolor the coat. If cages are required, be sure they are smoothly finished and thoroughly washable. Soft shag or plush carpeting is an added luxury, but avoid hard-finish nylon or wool pile, which pulls hair out by the pawful.

Indoor cattery cages should be free of abrasive surfaces and should provide for all of kitty's needs.

BRUSH AND NAIL DAMAGE

Keep the nails clipped at home as well as at the show, especially on the hind feet, to prevent accidental coat damage by scratching. More long ruffs are lost to unclipped nails than to any other cause. It is wise to keep your long-hair free of mats all year, but especially during show season. Do not allow the tiniest mat to form in a show coat. Kitty will try to remove it herself, usually with disastrous results. Brushing is sure to break the fragile coat; combing is far more desirable. If you must brush, as in the case of most shorthairs, do so *carefully* and always use a soft real bristle brush. Never use a nylon brush on a show cat, whatever its breed or coat.

TEMPERATURE CONTROL

Cats who live in normal house temperature will shed their hair at their normal time, usually late spring or early summer, depending upon the area, elevation and seasonal change. Sudden extremes in temperature can, and frequently do, affect the show coat in mid-season. An unusually hot spell can cause the longhair show cat to drop its coat in two or three weeks regardless of the time of year. Whenever the house has to be overheated, relegate kitty to the far end of the house and close the door . . . or you may be going to the next cat show with a feline nudist. For the more affluent breeders with their air-conditioned thermostatically controlled catteries, we have only envy. Most of us, however, after paying vet bills, entry fees and travel expenses, cannot afford such season-controlled luxuries. Owners of condition-controlled catteries are cautioned not to go overboard. Temperatures should never be set to the extreme . . . never less than 65 degrees or more than 76 degrees.

Gr. Ch. Bayhorne Zenith of Azulita, a blue Persian male. Mrs. Dulcie Benbow, England, breeder. Mrs. Marvin Head, owner.

DISCOLORATION AND STAINING

Loss of hair is not the only disaster that can befall the lovely show coat. Care should be taken to avoid accidental discoloration. Excess licking can bring about rust spots on blacks, smokes and torties and can cause yellowing on white and silver coats. Too much direct sunlight—even sunlight through a window or sliding glass door—can discolor the coat and give it a rusty look. Most cats do not enjoy water, but some think it's more fun than catnip and will play with a dripping faucet for hours or lie in a moist bathtub or sink. Continued dampness will cause discoloration in most show cats, particularly blues, blacks and creams.

Cleanliness of quarters is another key factor in the preservation of the show coat. Fresh litter daily will help prevent urine and feces stains on pants hair and foot tufts. If paper is preferred over litter for sanitary pans, always use paper towels for light-colored coats to prevent news-

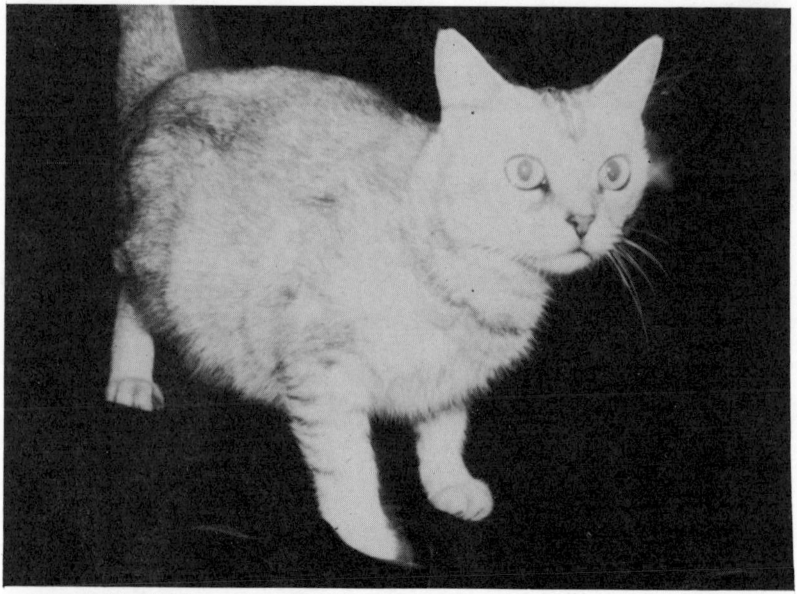

Norpark's Melba. Breeders Wayne P. Park and Kenneth E. Bender of Norpark Cattery, Elizabeth S. Freret.

Chanthaburi Aurora of Norpark. Irene Moore, breeder. Kenneth E. Bender, owner.

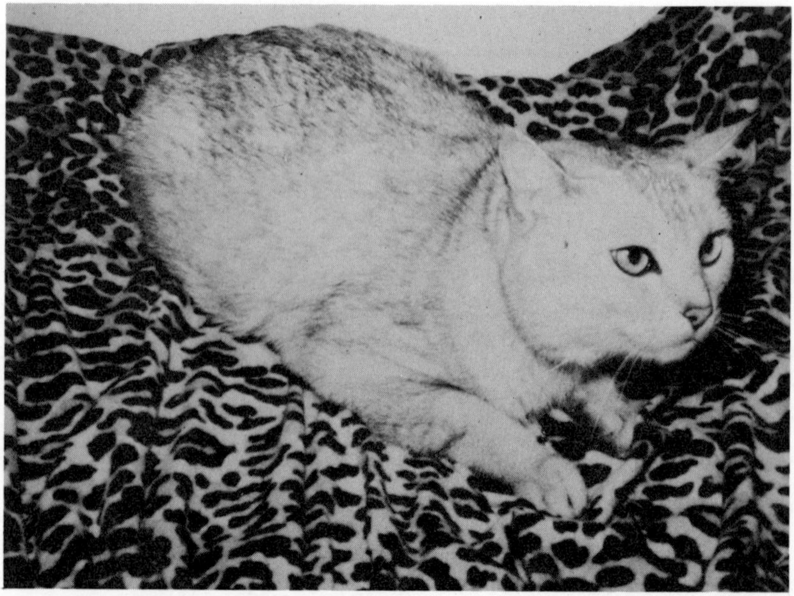

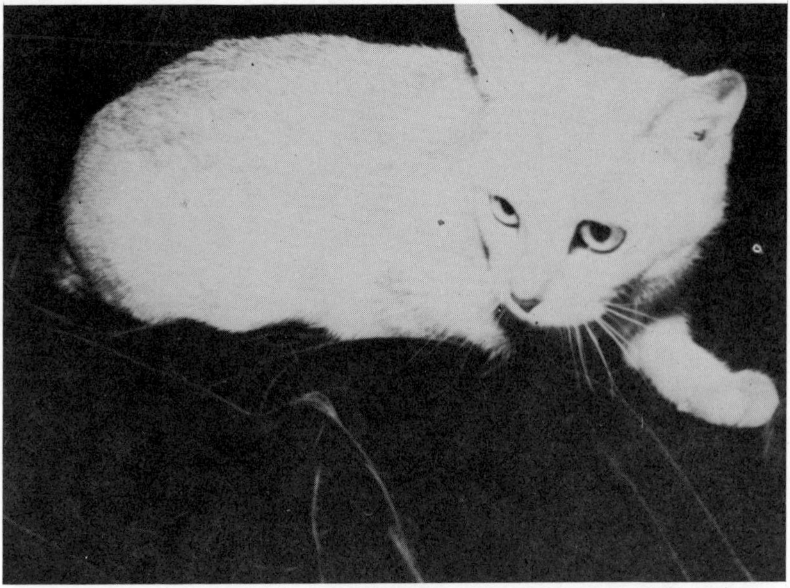

Ch. Shy-Ann's Amigo of Arca. Raymond Henke, breeder. Wayne Park and Rex Yale, owners.

Ch. Devi of Norpark. Wayne Park and Kenneth E. Bender, owners. (Devi is the dam of the first two CFA grand male Shaded Silver American shorthairs.)

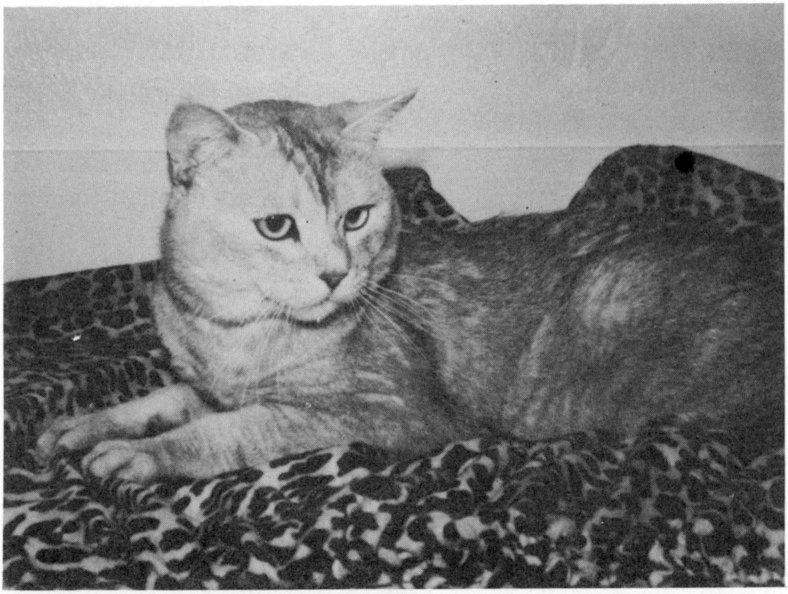

During mealtime a small baby's bib will prevent staining of the long ruff and save you a lot of extra grooming work.

print ink stain and the unnecessary darkening of foot pads. A fireplace screen will keep kitty out of the ashes and soot. Cat beds, bedding and carpeting must be vacuumed and/or laundered frequently to prevent the build-up of dust and dirt that soil the coat. During show season, if kitty is a sloppy eater, a small baby bib at mealtime will prevent food stains on the long ruff. Flat plates are recommended over bowls for the same reason.

If you confine your show cats to cage facilities, be sure to clean the walls and floors frequently. Spilled food, water, litter or just plain garden-variety grime can quickly spot a show coat. Wash food dishes and litter pans daily to prevent spot damage. Check with your veterinarian for non-toxic surface cleaners that cannot harm cats or kittens, then be sure to wipe the cage walls and floors dry before allowing the cats to re-enter. Cleanliness is not only a key factor to the good health of your animals but also vital to the preservation of the fragile show coat. Common sense is your good right hand—if you think something *might* damage the show coat, remove it!

6

TOUCH-UP GROOMING AT THE SHOW

After a long trip, the first thing on a traveler's mind is to refresh himself. He feels travel-weary and a bit dingy around the edges. A brief respite is in order—a trip to the bathroom, a quick clean-up, a few moments before the mirror and perhaps a light meal. The show cat can become travel-weary too and needs essentially the same sort of mental and physical retread in order to appear at her best.

The major grooming chores have been done at home. The coat is sparkling clean, each tiny mat removed, nails clipped, eyes and ears cleaned, excess powder blown from the coat, and a hundred and one small grooming tricks performed. Kitty's confinement to travel quarters, whether just across town or halfway across the state, has undoubtedly served to disarrange the most efficient grooming job. After having checked in with the Entry Clerk and received vet line approval, it is the time to check for "accidents" . . . *before* the judges arrive and *before* decorating the show cages. This will allow sufficient time to repair the damages, time to thoroughly cleanse any soiled areas, and time for kitty's long coat to dry after an unscheduled spot cleaning. Don't worry about the late-decorated cage. The judge isn't judging the cage, m'dear, he's judging the cat! There will be many unoccupied hours ahead in which to play interior decorator. Kitty's problems come first.

Barring car sickness and ill-timed accidents enroute, your cat should need only touch-up grooming at the show.

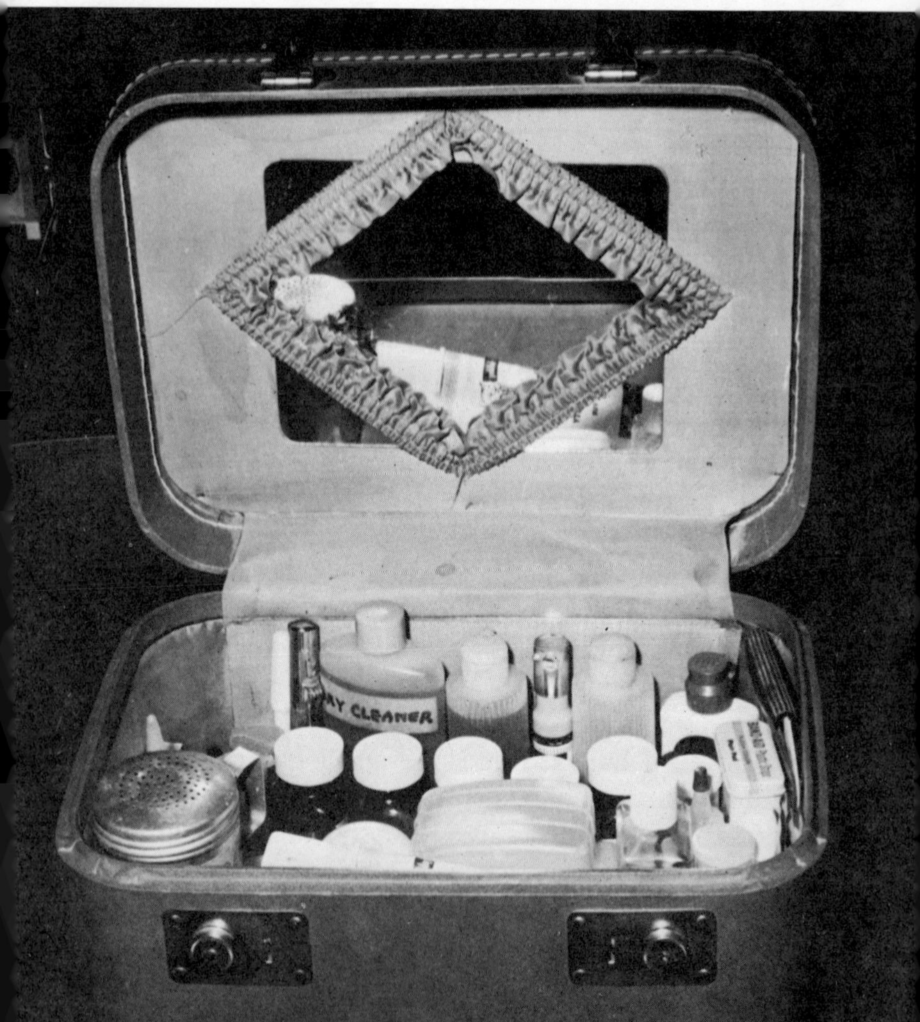

Your cat's traveling case should be roomy enough to carry all equipment for touch-up and emergency grooming at the show.

Check the various points mentioned under basic grooming. Never make the lazy mistake of thinking "I did that at home last night, so I won't bother checking today." It may not be a fatal mistake, but it is one that could cost you a win to another cat's owner who cared enough to doublecheck. Remember that every cat in competition is in there to *win*, and you must assume that each and every other breeder is pursuing that goal vehemently. If all points check out, all excess powder has been effectively removed and the coat is free from the smallest knot, you may begin the final comb.

COMBING AT THE SHOW

Repeat the combing procedures as detailed in Chapter 2, "Grooming The Longhair Cat." Begin by combing the face and chin with your *very fine* comb. The cheeks are combed forward and made to appear as full as possible. The top head and forehead are combed forward and down. The chin is combed forward and up toward the nose. Using the same comb, separate the fine long hair in the ears. The ear tufts are lifted and combed outward to cover as much of the ear opening as possible. On white Persians or smokes with pure white ear tufts, a touch of white grooming chalk will dry fine hair and aid in keeping it separate and full. The delicate grooming of the facial area is done before body combing for a sound reason. Holding a cat still for facial combing usually requires tucking kitty under your arm or placing a firm hand on her back for stability which, of course, crushes the coat and packs it closer to the body. Once combed, the face requires no further attention for an hour or so or until the next presentation to the judge.

Separate and pull the long toe tufts up between the cat's toes with your *very fine* comb. Since leg hair is short and fine and has a definite tendency to lay flat to the leg, switch to the *fine* comb and groom the legs with a firm

Comb the head area first, since the coat will be crushed from gripping the body.

upward motion. Brisk scrubbing with your small round shoe brush dipped in grooming powder will aid in last-minute fluffing and retaining body in the leg hair. Be sure to remove all signs of powder before presenting the cat to the judge. Comb up the leg from foot to body, taking care to comb all the way around and between the legs.

A *medium* comb is used on the body and on most of the ruff. The bib is combed upward over the broad chest and up under the chin. Then start in back of the shoulders to lift the hair up and out. Allow yourself plenty of time and work section by section. Travel can pack the lightest of coats. Reach deep into the coat, turning the comb slightly up and forward with the wrist action, working little by little the length of the back and down both sides toward the tail. Avoid contact, insofar as possible, with the base of the tail to prevent aggravation of the stud tail condition.

Shake the tail full by holding the tip upright in your fingers. Opinions are many and varied on tail grooming. Exhibitors have been seen back-brushing or reverse-combing the tail hair, presumably to add fullness, over-spraying and fan-combing. It is suggested that these practices be avoided or, if you must, kept to an absolute minimum to avoid damage to the long fragile tail hair. The pants hair is fluffed out with your *medium* comb, planting the comb deep and lifting upward and outward with each gentle stroke.

Finish touch-up combing by lifting the hair of the ruff out and upward toward the face and up and over the ears as far as possible. A final upward lift of the bib once more and kitty is ready to be carried to the judge. A body-inducing spray may be used as a final touch, but allow the coat to dry before lifting the cat from the grooming table.

An example of good show grooming demonstrated by Dbl. Gr. Ch. Zoda Rose Parade of La Cresta.

Proper handling is as important as good grooming. One hand is firmly placed under and between the front legs, the other supporting the rear.

CARRYING THE COMBED CAT

Carrying your cat to the judge sounds like an anti-climax to grooming. Do not be misled. Proper handling is almost as important as the grooming itself. The longhair cat is lifted carefully, one hand under and between the front legs, the other supporting the back legs. Do not crush the cat against your clothing or press your arms against its sides. Try, insofar as possible, to keep your arms akimbo with the cat in a protected position before your body. Frightened cats or first-show cats may, of necessity, require a firmer grip. In this case, try one hand under the chest supporting the cat, the cat's hips held against your side with the arm and elbow. The other hand supports and holds the cat's front feet together. The nervous cat gains great security in having the front paws firmly supported rather than left dangling.

The knowledgeable Steward will have left the back door of the judging cage open for your convenience. (Tip to Show Managers: instruct your Stewards to observe this courtesy.) Inspect the floor of the cage before placing the cat inside. Make certain that the between-cat disinfectant has been mopped dry with paper towels, that the male next door has not sprayed into your cage, and that the front door is securely latched. Many a cat has been safely deposited in the back door of a judging cage only to escape out of the front and disappear amid the Sunday crowd. All in order, lift your cat carefully into the cage. Hold him about three or four inches off the floor and *drop him!* The air generated by his descent will put a final fluff in the coat and, hopefully, lift any crushing that has occurred during your journey from grooming space to judging cage. Latch the door, say a reassuring word or two to your furry friend, and take your seat before the judging table.

"Big City" cat shows frequently draw a large crowd of paid spectators. God bless them, they help pay the bills. They are, however, a pain in the powder puff when you are

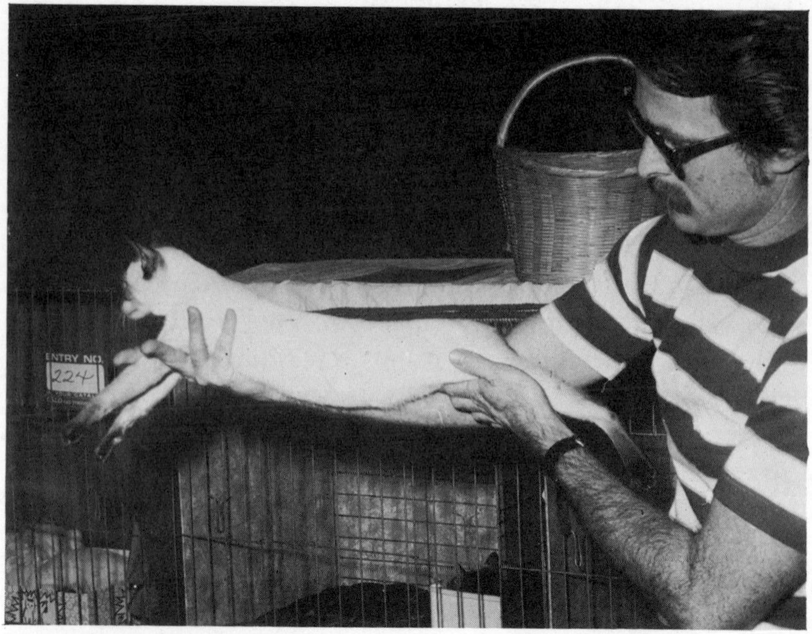

The stretched carry, demonstrated by UCF Judge Edward Bowers, is more practical for the shorthaired cat. Nervous cats should be held against one's side and their front paws firmly supported.

trying to navigate safely from show cage to judging cage. Crowded aisles with shoulder-to-shoulder Sunday visitors sometimes make your route to the judging area an obstacle course that would do justice to a Marine D.I. You have just spent twenty minutes lifting that luxurious coat to unforeseen heights, and halfway down the aisle an enthusiastic visitor reaches out of nowhere and runs a lotioned hand from ear tufts to tail. People crowd in around you and press the cat against your clothing. You are jostled and bumped until you feel like the number one ball in a pinball machine . . . and kitty looks like you left your combs at home. There is no real solution to crowded aisles except, perhaps, to take the line of least resistance, the long way around if there are fewer people in the way. *If* your cats are calm, and *if* you are tall enough to make it effective, you might experiment with the Skyway To The Judge. When necessity demands, cats are transported at the tops of raised arms, over the heads of the crowd, and out of temptation's reach. This is not the "best way to fly" for the average cat, however, and certainly not recommended for the novice exhibitor.

SPOT CLEANING AT THE SHOW

There will be many times in your cat's show career when he will inadvertently soil himself during the show. Emergency spot cleaning is in order, and the exhibitor should come prepared. We have found liquid Labco Dry Cleaner particularly effective. Moisten a pre-dampened sponge with Labco and carefully wipe the soiled area clean. Apply talcum powder to aid in rapid drying, then comb. (No powder on blacks or smokes, please!) If Listerine or similar product is used, allow a full ten minutes to dry before combing. If the soiled area is too extensive for emergency spot cleaning, you may have to take kitty to the

UCF Judge George Silva uses chamois on a shorthair before judging.

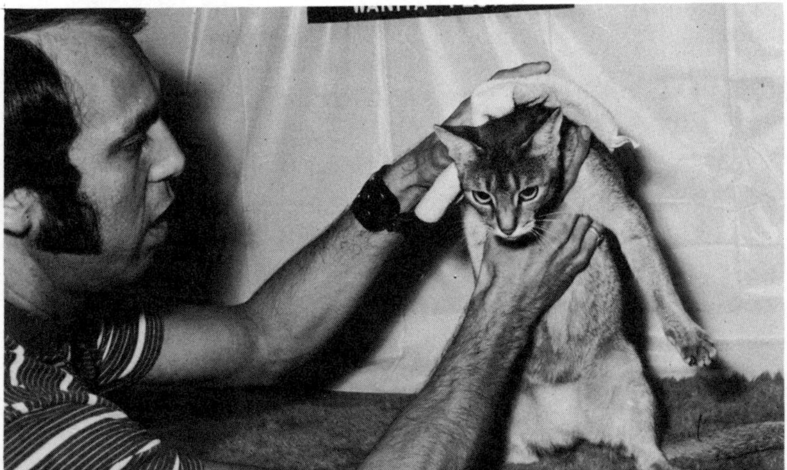

restroom. And take a friend along too, four hands are better than two. She can carry a towel, the hand hair dryer and a LONG extension cord. Rinse the soiled area with cold water, press the excess water out with an absorbent towel, dry it with the hair dryer, then powder and comb out. During your next touch-up grooming session, spray a little body-inducing spray on the cleansed area to give it a bit more body. Let it dry, then lift with a comb as usual. But a word of caution: a little spray goes a long way. Too much spray will make a coat sticky; used too often, it will dry the coat and cause it to lack luster. It is only the superfine hair or limp coat which benefits from such preparations.

Another particularly fine dry cleaner (for whites, blues and all colors using grooming powder) is Psssst, a dry spray shampoo manufactured by Clairol, which works absolute miracles to remove last-minute food stains from the ruff or sticky oily spots on the coat. It is also good for m'lady should she get up Sunday morning with her hair looking as if she, personally, had been in a cat fight. Spray the powder-like dry cleaner directly on the soil spot—watch the eyes!—let it dry three minutes and comb out.

Don't forget to groom those hidden places which can be the cause of embarrassing moments.

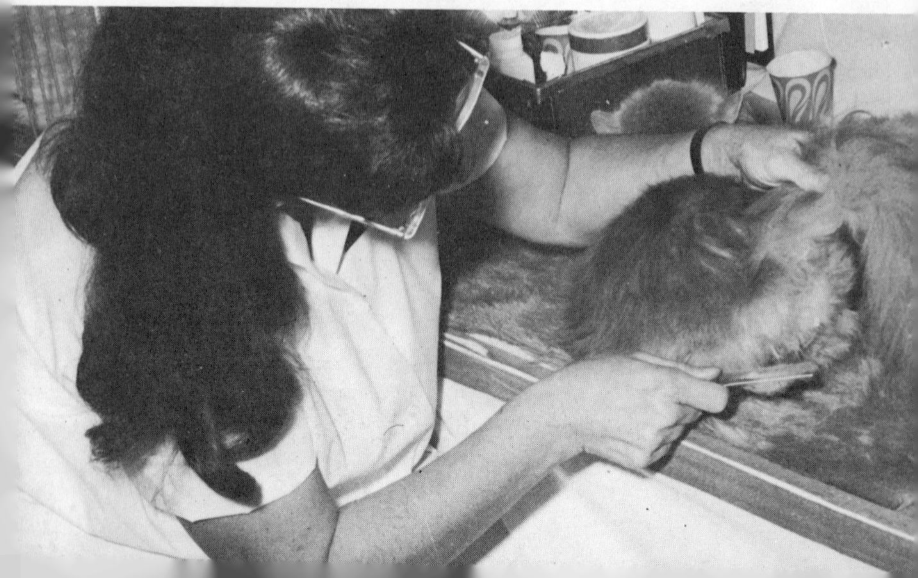

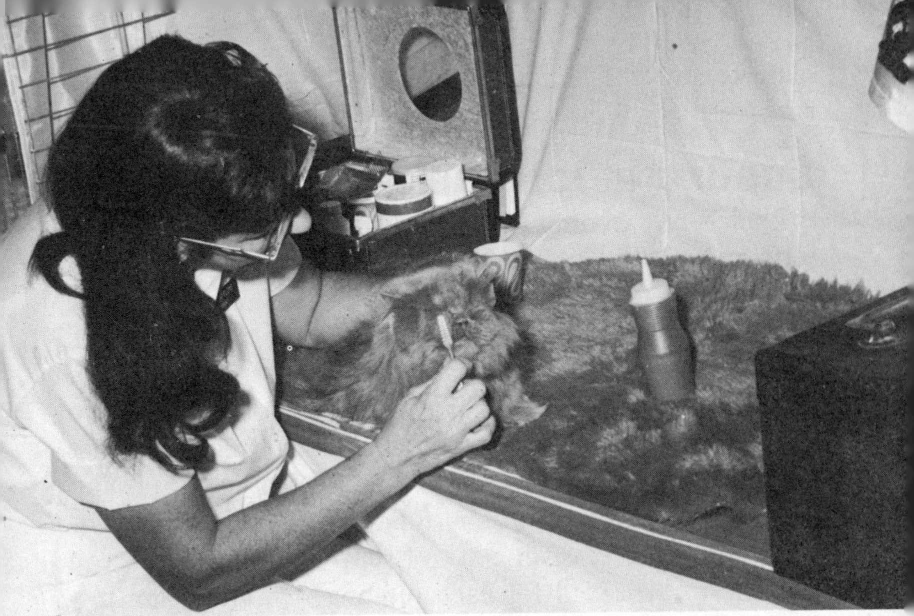
Should your cat dirty her face between showings, a little spray of a product like Psssst can work miracles.

Cornmeal is frequently used to clean the shorthair coat, by working it well in and through the coat, then brushing it gently out.

SPOT PREVENTION

To avoid many of these last-minute emergencies, keep a *clean* litter pan in your show cage, the back seat of your car and in your motel room. Avoid those intriguing under-the-strange-bed explorations by kitty, who inevitably un-earths a lazy maid's hidden sins and comes out looking like a lost chimney sweep.

Try to prevent excessive licking at the show. Many cats feel disarranged after combing and try to lick themselves neat again. A small lightweight baby bib will discourage compulsive licking in many cats; a small taste of Petromalt or bite of food changes the subject for others. Should kitty get his ruff in the water dish or otherwise dampen his coat, pat immediately with a towel, powder lightly and comb dry. Food given at or during the show should be given in very small portions, perhaps only a bite at a time, and on a flat plate to prevent accidental staining of the face hair and ruff.

GROOMING IS FOREVER

Touch-up grooming is suggested just prior to each judging call. The previous judge—if he has performed his duties well—will have ruffled the coat and handled the body to such an extent that re-grooming is a necessity. Accidents should be repaired immediately and never left until the next touch-up session. Judging schedules are subject to change, and you wouldn't want kitty to get caught with her pants powdered, would you? Watch your schedule and sequence of numbers on the judging stands. Begin touch-up grooming at least fifteen to twenty minutes before you are due to be called for each judging . . . and again just before the Finals are announced if you are properly optimistic.

Shorthair cats, of course, require different techniques both in grooming, touch-up grooming and methods of carry.

Touch-up grooming at the show is a simple matter for the shorthair owner. The ears and eyes are routinely checked to be sure they are immaculately clean, the face examined for food stains and the feet for soiled pads. The coat is ruffled backwards with a light sprinkling of grooming powder, *if used,* then brushed out with a very soft brush. A chamois or silk scarf is run lightly over the body to remove any lint or loose hair and to give the coat that finished appearance.

Certain shorthairs are carried from show cage grooming area to the judging cage in a "stretched" position . . . one hand beneath and between the front legs, the other beneath the tummy and just in front of the hind legs with the body gently taut between. The shorthair show cat should be trained to the stretch-carry at an early age, and every motion of show grooming and show judging should be simulated frequently as a part of the grooming ritual.

7

THE DON'TS OF SHOW GROOMING

There are as many rules governing the world of the cat show as there are in any other field of organized competition, be it human, mechanical or animal in origin. We assume that your cat is properly registered with an accurate pedigree, that you have entered the show in the proper class and in the proper manner. The "Don'ts of Show Grooming" to which we now refer are those candidly known as *cheating.*

The quickest way for the novice exhibitor to find himself permanently outside the "inside group" is to attempt to deceive the judges and claim undeserved wins. When the deception is discovered, and it will be discovered, your cat is disqualified. At the discretion of the sponsoring club, you may be barred from future shows with *any* cat. Legal facts aside, you will find little pleasure and no friendly admiration in the trophy won by deceit. Believe in your cat and have confidence in your ability to show it well. Play it square. Time and experience will bring you honest wins.

DYEING OR BLEACHING

Avoid the use of any dye or bleach. The chemical composition of the human body differs greatly from that of the feline. Hair dyes, rinses, bleaches and shampoo lighteners are chemically designed to change the color of the human hair strand. The effect of that same product upon the chemical structure of the cat hair usually results in total

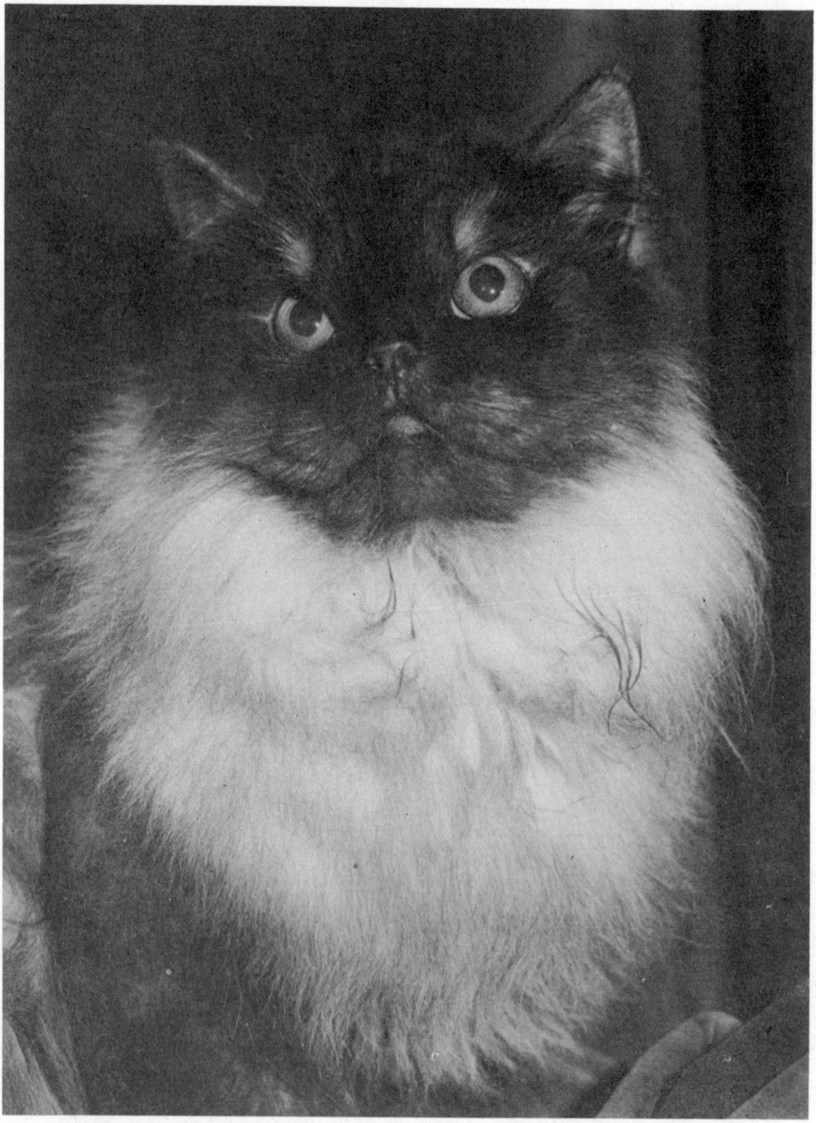

Gr. Ch. La Marque's Angel Puss, a Black Smoke Persian female. Breeder, Wanita Floyd; owner Robert W. Floyd.

disaster. The cat hair is finer and infinitely more fragile. The harsh chemicals in human hair products dry the cat hair and cause it to become brittle and strawlike in texture. So strong are these irritants that they will burn a cat's sensitive skin, kill the hair follicle and disrupt the flow of natural skin oils so necessary to a fur-bearing animal. Toxic by nature to the feline system, the use of dyes and dye-oriented products could result in the ultimate death of the animal upon which it was used. It is somewhat anti-climactic to inject at this point that human hair dyes will not accomplish the color change sought. You will merely acquire discolorations, streaking and crumpled split ends. Aside from the obvious dangers of dyes, bleaches and related products, the attempt represents grounds for immediate disqualification.

Judges handle thousands of cats and are well aware when some-one tries to tamper with a cat's coat.

COLORED CHALKS AND POWDERS

The use of colored chalk and colored powder to alter or mask poor color in a show cat is *strictly forbidden.* While non-toxic chalks and colored powders may not injure the animal, they are easily recognized by the judge as he moves his hands over the face, body and ruff. A residue of colored powder falls on the judging table, damp from repeated disinfecting between cats, and the judge picks up noticeable signs of color. Such flagrant violation of cat fancy standards is also grounds for disqualification.

EXCESS POWDER

Excess use of talcum or grooming powder is sternly frowned upon. The use of powder to pack the coat before a show, to dry excess oils and separate fine hair is a commonly

Love is very important to the proper development of the cat. Love the cat more than the win.

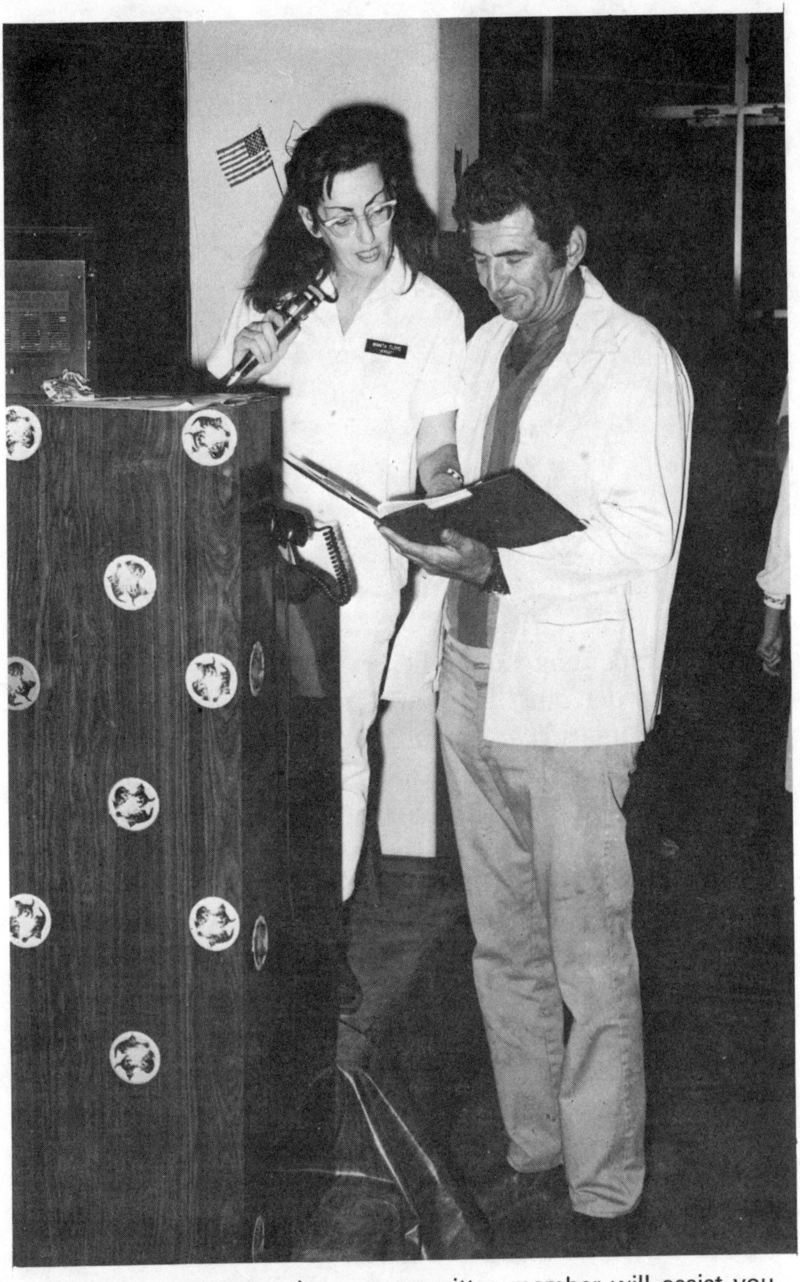

If you have any questions, a committee member will assist you.

Dbl. Ch. La Cresta's Ajaia, a white Persian neuter, is proud of his trophies. Breeder Betty Meins; owner Sandra Ambrose.

accepted grooming aid. Judicious use is stressed, however, and all powder must be blown or brushed out of the coat before presentation at the judging ring. Too much powder left in the coat is assumed to be an attempt at lightening the color or masking a color problem. It is left to the discretion of the judge whether the amount of powder in the coat constitutes disqualification. The use of excess powder in and around the ears is expressly forbidden. Heartless owners of cats with oversize ears sometimes force or blow powder deep into the ear opening just before judging call to bring the ear down and cause it to appear closer to the head. The action is painful to the animal and will result in eventual loss of hearing and infection. Powdering the ear canal is a deliberate attempt to deceive the judge and may result in disqualification.

PERFUMED PRODUCTS

The use of perfume or perfumed products on the show animal is a matter of *personal preference*. It is suggested that the exhibitor consider the fact that most talcums are scented, and a noticeable scent on the show cat *might* indicate, to a stickler-for-the-rules judge, that this particular cat is too highly powdered. Unscented powders are recommended for show use. Scented products, however, are a luxury we may all indulge in with delight at home.

Looking forward to next season is Dbl. Gr. Ch. La Marque's Greek Smoke, black smoke Persian male. Breeder Wanita Floyd; owner Robert W. Floyd.

COLORED PENCILS AND EYE PRODUCTS

The use of colored pencils and eye products to intensify markings *is also forbidden.* Silver Persians, as an example, have a rim of dark pigmentation around their eyes, nose and mouth. This mascara-like outline of the features gives the cat a hauntingly beautiful expression. The lack of this pigmentation is a fault in the show cat and temptation frequently lies in using black eyebrow pencil. The use of brown pencils and eye make-up has been tried on brown tabbies, Abyssinians, Himalayans and Siamese for various purposes. Waterproof black mascara was used by one unscrupulous breeder of blacks to mask a spot of light undercoat and by another to enhance the butterfly markings of a silver tabby. The *only* colored pencil products accepted by the cat fancy are those white chalks used to cover eye stains on a white cat. Any use other than white-on-white constitutes an attempt to deceive the judge by artificial means, and disqualification may result.

PLUCKING

The plucking of white spots, live guard hair and tabby markings is considered a deliberate attempt to alter the coat of the show animal. Guard hair is somewhat longer and slightly darker than the rest of the coat. Cat show judges are fully aware of the existence of guard hair, and the cat who does not possess it is immediately suspect. The owner who removes live guard hair in an attempt to insure a sound color coat is breaking one of the basic rules. The removal of dead guard hair, the occasional stray white hairs from a dark coat, and the single white or discolored whisker is permitted. Food-stained or water-rusted tips on the bib or ruff may also be removed as instructed in previous chapters. These are not faults in the cat but a matter of good grooming. Never attempt to pluck a white locket of hair or to remove bars or tabby markings from your cat. Such actions can only be interpreted as a deliberate attempt to alter the coat color.

PENALTIES FOR CHEATING

There are tricks to every trade, and the judges are aware of them all. They know when the Abyssinian breeder uses urine to darken a white patch or locket. They notice when the Havana Brown owner uses brown eye make-up to conceal a light spot in an otherwise faultless coat. They recognize the use of black-and-white newsprint rubbed carefully over the back of the Shaded Silver Persian to intensify the tipping. They know there's chicanery in the cattery when a Siamese tail has been cunningly shaved to effect that close-to-the-body look. Every color and breed of show animal has undoubtedly, at one time or another, been the victim of an unwise owner's duplicity. *Fortunately, these persons make up a very small minority in the cat fancy.* Their identity is usually known by their competitors but, even more important, they are recognized by the judges and mentally dismissed from Final Wins consideration. Seldom will a cat-show judge call out an offender before the crowd. Cat shows are pleasant busy weekends run on a tight schedule, and an open accusation would only disrupt the show and discredit the cat fancy before the public. The cat's number is mentally noted for later investigation and the cat disregarded for more than cursory ribbons which he would have won despite the attempt at fraudulence. The offender may rest assured, however, the judge will check the show catalog after the Finals to see which cattery would indulge in such questionable tactics. Their identity is not soon forgotten.

The phrase "honesty is the best policy" is more than a cliche; it's a way of life among reputable catteries. Allow *your* cat its full measure of fair competition and accept your wins, and your losses, with good grace. Deceit is the diet of fools.

Quad. Ch. La Cresta's Mardi Gras, a white Persian male. (Born 1960) Breeder/owner Betty Meins.

8

OFF-SEASON CARE OF THE SHOW CAT

No matter how much you enjoyed the busy show season, no matter how many trophies your cats won, the exhibitor always looks forward to the respite of the off-season. From mid-April until September, the cat owner can relax. At least that's what it says in the small print at the bottom of the page . . . but like most of those "small print" clauses, don't you believe a word of it! You have simply exchanged one set of duties for another.

Perhaps you don't travel to an out-of-town cat show every other weekend, but you find you can't resist driving a hundred miles east, west, north and south to see promising new show kittens for sale. Furthermore, there is the breeding program you planned: kittens to deliver, wean and sell; cats to clip down; new cage curtains to make; cat club meetings and the advance work on next season's show. Oh yes, of course, and a few moments for the family who—silly people—thought they were going to get your undivided attention now that summer is here. You find yourself caught in a whirlwind of cat-oriented activities you swore would never happen to you . . . and you're loving every minute of it. But don't worry, cats are contagious. First thing you know, everybody in the family will have his own show cat and will be running around just like you. Ask any breeder. It's a classic fact of the cat fancy.

PLANNED BREEDING

One of the first off-season chores is the initiation of a well-planned breeding program. The show female who is to be bred in the spring and shown again in the fall must, of necessity, become the object of immediate and careful planning. Plan early families for your show stock. Since the show coat will suffer noticeably from pregnancy and subsequent nursing, the breeder must allow sufficient time for the coat to restore itself. The pre-natal diet is chosen with care and well-laced with extra calcium and vitamin/mineral supplements specifically designed for the expectant feline. A proven stud male, whose show qualities complement those of the female, has been selected well in advance of the need. Plans are made for a breeding schedule wherein the delivery date will not conflict with vacation plans and visiting relatives. Care is taken to avoid over-

KMR, the new and improved Tabbi-Lac, will fulfill all of your kittens' needs should mama be unable to nurse.

The summer coat is short, but grooming should continue as before to maintain the grooming routine.

weight problems among breeding queens, for both conception and delivery are complicated by excess fat.

The unproven queen should be bred simultaneously with another female of proven milk supply to provide a wet nurse should kitty's first litter leave her high and *dry*. In an emergency, contact your vet or any large pet store for Tabbi-Lac, a canned pre-mixed cat milk formula which may be fed from a pet nurser bottle. The modus operandi of breeding season is, however, another book and reference is made herein for the purpose of properly scheduling your show cat's busy summer.

Gr. Ch. Zoda Bonanza, a cream Persian male. Sired by Zoda Frivolous of Pensford, Import. Dam is Fiddlers Green Valerie of Zoda. Zoe McEachern, breeder.

Gr. Ch. Honey Bear's Danny Boy, a shaded silver Persian male. Ann M. Giuffre, breeder and owner.

SUMMER EXERCISE

Exercise schedules vary only slightly in the summer months. For a brief period while the old coat is shedding out and the new coat has not yet made a noticeable appearance, kitty may relax and romp unrestrained with her feline friends. Outdoor exercise cages or runs should be suitably shaded to prevent sun-rusting of the new coat as it grows in. Indoor or caged cats should be provided with the means of active daily exercise. Regularly hold the cat up between you and the light to see if the first thin scattering of new guard hair extending an inch or more above the short summer coat has made its appearance. When it is detected, curtail group rough-housing and play time. The new fragile coat is easily damaged and must be protected if kitty is to be ready for the fall show season.

SUMMER GROOMING

Off-season grooming is a job somewhat lessened but unavoidable. There is a natural tendency in the hot summer months to let things slide. It is very easy to acquire knots on the "*mañana* plan." Every day they become a little larger and every day you promise yourself to remove them *mañana*. The show season is a whole three months away. *Mañana*. Then suddenly you have an unsalvageable mat and a hole in the incoming show coat big enough—you should pardon the pun—to throw a cat through. Don't let it happen to you. Weekly combing should suffice during the summer months, accompanied by light powdering to prevent mats and keep kitty accustomed to his old grooming routine. While baths are seldom necessary during the off-season, flea powder becomes doubly important. Summer is flea season and your pet's worst time with those bloodsucking little parasites. The application of a good cat flea powder should become a part of your weekly grooming routine, more often if required.

During off-season shedding, the best show coat will appear ragged and unkempt.

CLIPPING CONTROVERSY

Clipping the longhair show cat is one of the most controversial subjects in the cat fancy. It is a decision only the breeder can make. There are good arguments in favor of spring clipping. It eliminates the major grooming chores, the cats remain cool and comfortable despite the heat, and the new coat comes in fresh, full and evenly colored. And there are equally good arguments against the issue of clipping: slow regrowth of hair; the unpredictability of coat length for the first shows of the season; and the possibility of a traumatic effect on shy or easily frightened cats. Generally speaking, it has been found to be an individual problem with each cat. Some respond with quick regrowth and fabulous coats, while others show little or no improvement. If your show cat has a poor, off-color coat and split or damaged hair, certainly clipping should do it no harm, and it might improve the coat quality immeasurably. The period of regrowth is unpredictable. Instruction is offered in the proper method of clipping your longhair show cat, but the decision is yours.

CLIPPING EQUIPMENT

Longhair cats may be clipped at most veterinarian offices. Your explicit instructions on what to clip and what not to clip will be followed. Or you may do the job at home with a good pair of Oster Animal Clippers and the assistance of an understanding friend. *Never* attempt to use human hair clippers on your cat. The texture of cat hair is such that it binds in the human clipper blades and will pull, not cut, the cat's long coat. Assemble all items needed: Oster Animal Clippers; Oster #5 blade (which cuts $\frac{3}{4}$ to 1 inch above the skin); Oster #10 blade (clips $\frac{1}{4}$ inch from the skin: used primarily for removing severe mats); a liquid blade cooling preparation; and a can of Johnson's *Medicated* Baby Powder. The cooling preparation is sold wherever animal clipper blades are sold and is used to lubricate and cool the blades and to prevent razor burns on sensitive skin. Check the clipper blades every minute or two by placing them against the inside of your wrist, as you would check a baby bottle. If too warm, allow the blades to cool and respray before resuming clipping operations.

CLIPPING PROCEDURE

Begin clipping with the least tender parts of the cat's body, the back and sides. One person holds the cat motionless on a table of convenient working height, while the second person clips from shoulders to tail following the

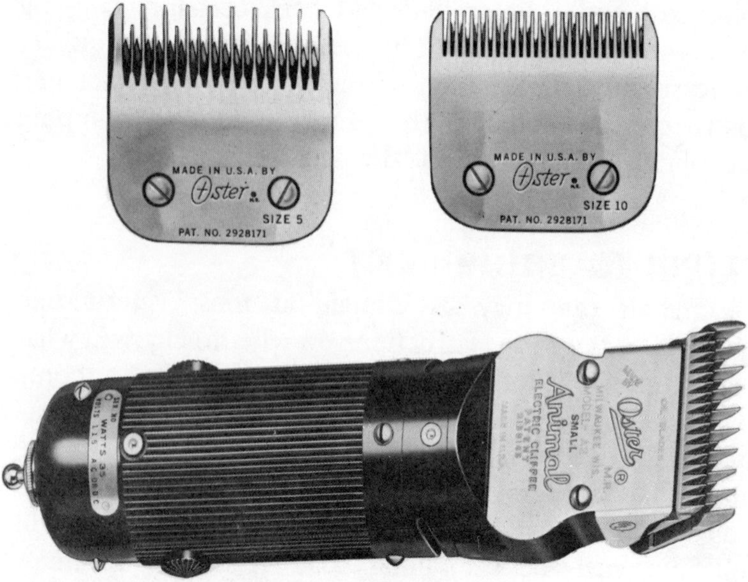

Always use an animal clipper (never human) should you need to clip your cat's coat. Shown are Oster Small Animal Clippers with #5 and 10 blades.

natural lie of the hair. The skin is held as taut as possible with the flat of the left hand, moving just ahead of the clippers. Work from shoulders to base of tail, and from sides down to flanks. Then, with your assistant supporting the cat in the air, hind feet resting on the table, carefully clip the stomach area. Keep the skin taut ahead of the clipper blade and remember to check the blades against your wrist every minute or so. Extreme caution must be used when clipping the stomach to avoid injuring the small nipples hidden in the deep hair. Clip the back of the hind legs and pants hair *only* if absolutely necessary.

Do not clip the legs, feet, ruff, head or tail. *Never* clip a longhair's tail unless there is absolutely no alternative. If it must be shaved or clipped to remove mats, a curse on the owner's head for allowing it to get in that condition! These areas seem to require twice as long to regrow, and unnecessary clipping may curtail your cat's show career for an entire season.

GROOMING THE CLIPPED LONGHAIR

The transition from long coat to summer butch haircut requires certain common sense care on the part of the

Always follow the natural lie of the hair when clipping; check the clipper for overheating to prevent razor burns.

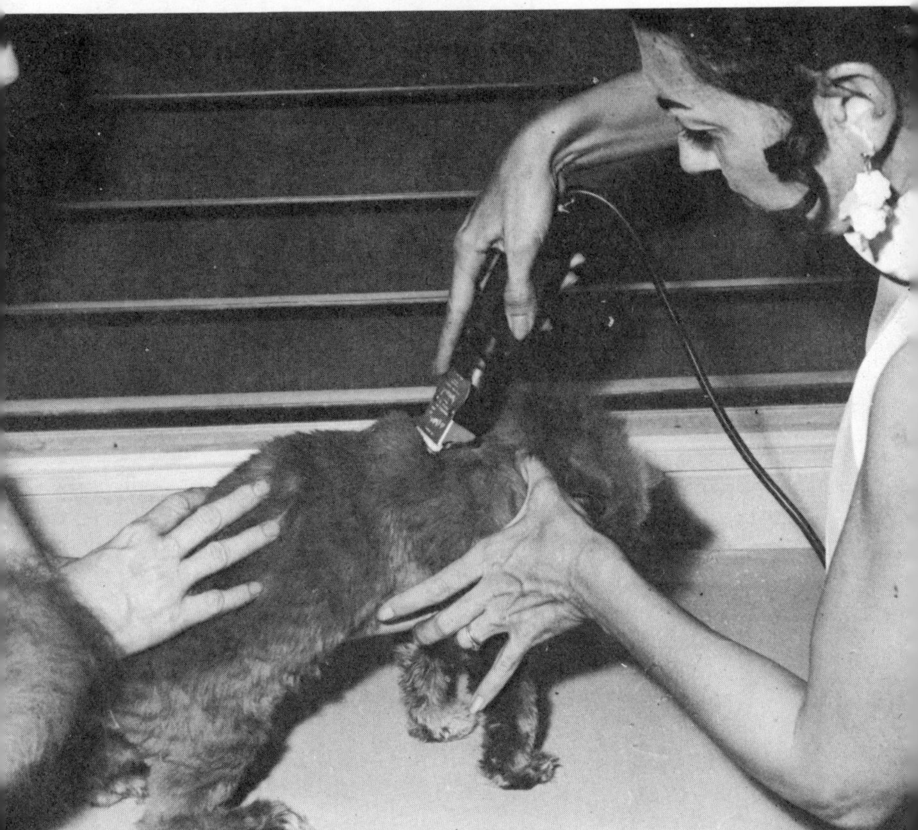

cattery owner. An unexpected late spring cold spell could easily chill the clipped cat. The use of a cat sweater or warm bed box is suggested for outdoor catteries or chilly nights to prevent colds and respiratory problems. Most pet stores carry light cat sweaters or a sleeve off one of your old sweaters can be quickly converted for cat use.

Your lovely longhair, now clipped to resemble a small lion, faces the hot summer months in cool comfort. Johnson's Medicated Baby Powder is recommended after clipping for a soothing, sweet-scented finishing touch. The clipped cat requires little combing—only the ruff, legs and tail—but token grooming should be continued on a regu-

Gr. Ch. Brentwood's Prince Nickie of Honey Bear, a shaded silver Persian male. Sophia A. Wyborny, breeder. Ann M. Giuffre, owner. A near-perfect example of face grooming.

larly scheduled basis to preserve the habits of good grooming behavior.

PLANNED SUMMER VACATIONS

Family vacations should be scheduled in advance to coincide with your cat-sitter's availability. Advise your veterinarian of your planned absence and authorize emergency treatment as needed for the cats you leave behind. Remember to prepare a route-and-time schedule where you may be reached along the way and a written *detailed* list of instructions for care and feeding at home. Leave a spare key with a friend or neighbor in case the cat-sitter loses the key in your absence. Check window screens, gas pilot lights and wedge doors that slam. Better safe than sorry.

Your major off-season chores completed, you can relax and enjoy your cats . . . until the time for kitty's annual pre-season veterinarian check-up and booster shots.

We have tried to reveal a few of the heretofore whispered trade secrets of good grooming. Armed with the basic knowledge of proper grooming techniques, you can face your first cat show with a certain degree of confidence. If we have repeated ourselves throughout the book, it was with purposeful intent. Repetition improves retention, and important points *must* be retained. Good health is important to your cat's appearance as well as his physical survival. Frequent and good grooming habits are vital to his show career and to his daily comfort. Never, but *never*, lose sight of the cardinal rule of the cat fancy . . . love the cat, not the win.

Index

For ease of recognition, championship titles earned by cats listed in the following index have not been used.

E

F

G

H

I

K

L

M

N

O

P